# CREEKS & HARBOURS OF THE
# SOLENT
## NEEDLES TO CHICHESTER

# CREEKS & HARBOURS OF THE
# SOLENT
## NEEDLES TO CHICHESTER

## K. ADLARD COLES

## Eleventh Edition

**Adlard Coles Nautical**
London

Eleventh edition 1992

Published by Adlard Coles Nautical
an imprint of A & C Black (Publishers) Ltd
35 Bedford Row, London WC1R 4JH

© K. Adlard Coles 1992

| | |
|---|---|
| First Published | 1933 |
| Second Edition | 1936 |
| Reprinted | 1939 |
| Third Edition | 1946 |
| Fourth Edition | 1948 |
| Fifth Edition | 1954 |
| Sixth Edition | 1959 |
| Seventh Edition | 1963 |
| Eighth Edition | 1972 |
| Reprinted | 1973 |
| Ninth Edition | 1981 |
| Tenth Edition | 1987 |

ISBN 0–7136–3419–7

A CIP catalogue record for this book is available from
the British Library.

Typeset in Monophoto Sabon by
August Filmsetting, Haydock, St Helens

Printed in Great Britain by
Richard Clay Ltd, Bungay, Suffolk

Caution
While great care has been taken in the compilation of
this book, it is regretted that neither the authors nor the
publishers can accept responsibility for any inaccuracies or
mishaps arising from the work.

# Contents

# Index Map

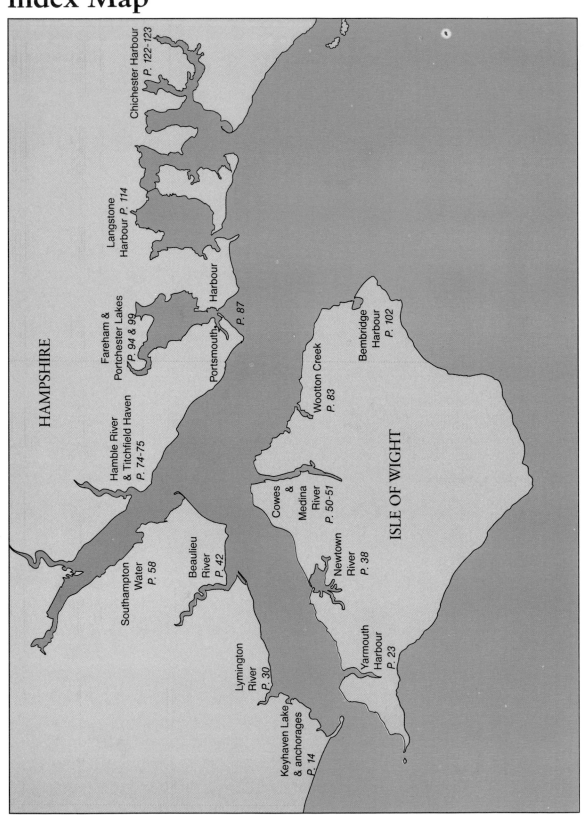

HAMPSHIRE

Chichester Harbour *P. 122-123*

Langstone Harbour *P. 114*

Fareham & Portchester Lakes *P. 94 & 99*

Portsmouth Harbour *P. 87*

Hamble River & Titchfield Haven *P. 74-75*

Southampton Water *P. 58*

Beaulieu River *P. 42*

Lymington River *P. 30*

Keyhaven Lake & anchorages *P. 14*

Wootton Creek *P. 83*

Bembridge Harbour *P. 102*

Cowes & Medina River *P. 50-51*

Newtown River *P. 38*

Yarmouth Harbour *P. 23*

ISLE OF WIGHT

# Preface and Acknowledgements for the 11th Edition

*The Creeks of the Isle of Wight* by K. Adlard Coles, already author of *Close Hauled* and *In Broken Water*, was published by The Yachtsman Publishing Co Ltd in 1928 at the price of two shillings. It was followed by the first edition of *Creeks and Harbours of the Solent*, published by Edward Arnold & Co in 1933. That edition did not include Langstone or Chichester harbours, but it set a style that remained popular with yachtsmen for thirty years. Sadly, Adlard Coles has died. He was, by the end of his life, the author of some eighteen books on sailing, including such classics as *Heavy Weather Sailing* and *Channel Harbours & Anchorages*. His last work was his autobiography, *Sailing Years*. His early book, *Close Hauled* has just been issued in paperback.

Now we have the eleventh edition of *Creeks and Harbours of the Solent*. It is just over sixty years since the first edition and it seems appropriate to re-print the following two paragraphs from the preface to that first edition.

'The name "The Solent" applies to the belt of sea between the mainland and the Isle of Wight. The Venerable Bede, 637–735, the first accredited recorder of written history of England, states that "The Island is situated opposite the division (Southampton Water) between the South Saxons and the Gewissoe, being separated from it by a Sea, three miles over, which is called Solente," He speaks also of the River Hamble, which he calls "Homelea" (see also Camden's *Britannia*, by William Gibson, London, 1695; also 2nd edition, 1722.)

'So again the Director-General of the Ordnance Survey: "The Solent applies to the belt of sea between Hurst Castle and the Needles to Southsea Castle and Bembridge Foreland, 'Spithead' applies to the roadstead at the eastern end of the Solent extending about two miles N.W. and S.E. along the south-west side of the Spit Sand, from Gillicker Point to Spit Fort, with an average breadth of one and a half miles."

The most noticeable change in this eleventh edition is the introduction of completely new charts. These should be clearer in use, and conform closely with both Admiralty charts and those produced by publishers specializing in yachtsmen's charts. However it must still be stressed that a current chart of the area should be used in conjunction with this pilot, as with any other. Many of the photographs are also new, and the *Approaches to the Solent* section will hopefully be of value to those entering for the first time.

The pace of development in this, the most popular sailing ground in Europe, is rapid and it is inevitable that changes will have taken place between research and publication. Observations concerning changes, errors or improvements which should be incorporated in future editions will be gratefully received by the publishers.

Much of the early research for this edition was carried out by Peter Coles in his capacity as Editor of Nautical Books. Following the amalgamation of that imprint with Adlard Coles in 1991 to form Adlard Coles Nautical, further checking and updating was carried out by Anne Hammick and members of the Adlard Coles Nautical team prior to publication.

Grateful thanks are due to the many harbourmasters, yacht club officials and others who have freely contributed their knowledge in the compilation of this new edition. In particular: Mr Tom Holt, River Warden, Keyhaven; Mr N. G. Ward, Harbour Master, Yarmouth; Mr Fred Woodford, Harbour Master, Lymington: Mr K. B. A. Abernethy, Harbour Master, Newtown; Mr W. Grindey, Harbour Master, Beaulieu: Captain H. N. J. Wrigley, Harbour Master, Cowes: Mr W. G. Pritchett, Harbour Master, Newport; Captain M. J. Ridge, Harbour Master, and Mr C. W. Mott, Moorings Officer, Southampton; Mr A. J. Ward, Creekmaster, Ashlett Creek; Captain C. J. Nicholl OBE, Harbour Master, River Hamble; Mr S. Reucroft, Hon Secretary, Hill Head Sailing Club; Mr R. W. Perraton, Hon Secretary, Wootton Creek Fairway Association; Captain J. Chestnutt, Queen's Harbour Master, and Mr R. F. Collyer, Port Surveyor, Portsmouth; Mr M. H. Coombes, General Manager, Bembridge Harbour Improvements Co Ltd; Captain P. Hansen, Harbour Master, Langstone Harbour, and Captain J. A. H. Whitney, Harbour Master, Chichester Harbour. Also to John Cunningham-Reid, who loaned his yacht tender to a complete stranger bent on investigating his home waters of Chichester Harbour.

The Solent is one of the most enjoyed and valued stretches of water in Europe. It is also under constant threat from industrial and commercial development. The New Forest District Council and The Solent Preservation Society, together with the authorities on the Isle of Wight, Work hard to protect its interests. Please support any action to keep these waters as pleasant as they are.

# Explanation of Terms and Sailing Directions

## Abbreviations.

| | | | | | |
|---|---|---|---|---|---|
| EC | Early Closing | Fl | Flashing | Oc | Occulting |
| CD | Chart Datum | G | Green | PO | Post Office |
| HW | High Water | Gp | Group | Q | Quick |
| LW | Low Water | H, horiz | Horizontal | R | Red |
| LAT | Lowest Astronomical Tide | h, m | Hours, minutes | S | Stripes |
| MHWS | Mean High Water Springs | IoW | Isle of Wight | s, sec | seconds |
| MHWN | Mean High Water Neaps | IQ | Interrupted Quick | SC | Sailing Club |
| MLWS | Mean Low Water Springs | Iso | Isophase | VQ | Very Quick |
| MLWN | Mean Low Water Neaps | IVQ | Interrupted Very Quick | V, vert | Vertical |
| B | Black | L Fl | Long Flashing | W | White |
| Bn | Beacon | M | Miles | Y | Yellow |
| Cheq | Chequered | m | metres | YC | Yacht Club |
| Dn | Dolphin | Mag | Magnetic | | |
| F | Fixed | NB | Notice Board | | |

**Chart Datum.** The datum of the charts in this edition is approximately LAT, which for practical purposes is the lowest predicted tide, ignoring exceptional meteorological conditions. Lowering the datum to a level to which the tide rarely falls has the pessimistic result in the Solent of showing from 0.5 to 0.6 m less water than formerly when the chart datum was approximately at the level of MLWS (Mean Low Water Springs). Many minor creeks useful for shoal draft craft are now shown as drying out. In order to clarify the position, the tidal heights above chart datum are given at the head of each chapter and it is necessary only to add the appropriate figure to arrive at depths at MLWS and MLWN.

In the text where references are made to low water, the abbreviation CD (chart datum) is frequently added to emphasize the point that there will be more water at MLWS, which is important when calculating depths over shallows. For example, where a depth at CD on part of the Hamilton Bank off Portsmouth is given as 0.6 m, reference to the tidal heights indicates that, with the addition of the appropriate 0.6 m at MLWS, the depth will be doubled to 1.2 m and at MLWN there will be about 2.3 m, which is a very different matter.

**Beacons and Piles.** These are shown either as a small round O, or symbolized – as also are perches, but the latter have been omitted where the scale is too small.

**Bearings.** The bearings in degrees are true, but approximate bearings are expressed in magnetic points of the compass. Local variation in 1992 is about 5°W. The terms 'port' and 'starboard' refer to the side on which objects lie when the vessel is approaching from seaward.

**Sailing Directions.** Whilst great care has been taken that the sailing directions and the charts in this book should be accurate, the publishers and the author cannot accept any responsibility for any errors or omissions which may have escaped notice. The author would be glad to receive any information or suggestions relating to the areas covered by this book which readers may consider would improve the next edition: Letters should be addressed to the Editor, Adlard Coles Nautical, A & C Black Ltd, 35 Bedford Row, London WC1R 4JH.

The charts in this book are based on Admiralty charts and other authorities, by kind permission. They have been enlarged, altered and amplified to embody much information obtained by the author and other yachtsmen for the areas covered. It cannot, however, be too firmly emphasized that these charts are intended to supplement, and not to supersede, ordinary navigation charts. Admiralty charts are constantly being corrected, whereas corrections in a work of this kind can be made only on the occasion of a new edition. The following Admiralty charts will be useful to yachtsmen and others cruising in Solent waters:

No 2045  *Outer Approaches to the Solent*
No 2219  *Western Approaches to Solent*
No 2040  *Solent (western part)*
No 2021  *Harbours and Anchorages in the West Solent area*
No 2793  *Cowes Harbour and River Medina*
No 1905  *Southampton Water and Approaches*
No 2041  *Port of Southampton*
No  394  *Solent (eastern part)*
No 2625  *Approaches to Portsmouth*
No 2631  *Portsmouth Harbour*
No 2050  *Eastern Approaches to the Solent*
No 2022  *Harbours and Anchorages in the East Solent Area*
No 3418  *Langstone and Chichester harbours*

**Chart Convention**

One of the most immediately noticeable features of the new charts drawn for this edition is the radical change in colour convention. Land not covered by normal Spring Tides has been left white. Intertidal areas which dry at Chart Datum are depicted in grey. Areas which remain covered at Chart Datum are shown in blue tints with increasing density of colour used to indicate greater depths of water. Beyond the 10 m contour, solid colour is used and further increases in depth are shown by means of soundings.

**High Water.** Where there is double high water, as at Southampton at spring tides, constants on Portsmouth are given for both first and second high water. At other harbours, where there is a long stand of about 2 hours near high water, the constants are for mean HW.

**Lights.** Lights indicated by stars without legends or with incomplete legends represent two fixed lights arranged vertically and seen Red to port – Green to starboard, proceeding up-stream.

**Channel Marking.** It is a feature of many creeks described in this book that the course of the channel changes from year to year and the buoyage and leading marks are altered to suit. Thus their positions shown on the chartlets should be taken as approximate.

# Approaches to the Solent

**The Needles Channel**

Most yachts arriving from the south and south west will find the Needles Channel the most obvious route into the Solent. It is well buoyed and clearly lit at night, although one often feels that the Needles lighthouse could show a more imposing illumination. Extreme caution must be taken when a south westerly wind of anything over Force Four is blowing over an ebbing tide, since not only do the seas in the vicinity of the SW Shingles Buoy and the Bridge Buoy become steep and breaking, but strong gusts often occur due to the effect of the high cliffs at this end of the Isle of Wight. The area is best left alone in anything approaching a gale and either a change of plan to an alternative port such as Poole, or sheltered anchorage such as at Studland Bay, should be sought until the wind moderates.

The Shingles bank lies to the west of the channel and seas break heavily over it. Care should be taken on an early ebb, since the stream sets across the bank as it pours out from Hurst Narrows. The bank shifts, and after severe gales the occasional island has been known to appear! Best given a wide berth.

When approaching from a more southerly direction, the Needles Fairway RW vertically striped buoy (*L Fl 10s*) is a good sized and visible reference point. Steer 042° to pass between SW Shingles R Buoy (*Fl R 2.5s*) and the Bridge West Cardinal Buoy (*VQ (9) 10s*). Leave the Shingles Elbow R buoy (*Fl (2) R 5s*) and Mid Shingles R buoy (*Fl (3) R 10s*) well to port. Shape course to pass between Warden G Buoy (*Fl G 2.5s*) and the NE Shingles East Cardinal (*Q (3) 10s*) and thence continue in a north easterly direction to pass through Hurst Narrows and into the Solent.

Approaching Hurst from the westward near LW take care to avoid 'The Trap', a shingle bank extending three-quarters of a cable S (Mag) from the Round Fort with little water over it at CD. It is in the form of a gravel projection from the beach, steep on each side.

Rough water and strong tides will be encountered in Hurst Narrows and often a boat speed of over 6 knots is required to battle an adverse tide.

**North Channel and Shingles**

When sailing to the Solent from the west, the North Channel may be better than the Needles Channel and is considered safer in gales. Coming from the westward a yacht should be steered with Hurst High Light bearing 097° until the North Head G buoy (*Fl (3) G 10s*) is sighted. Then steer to leave it to starboard and round into the channel running SE parallel with Hurst Beach. This gives about 3.0 m at CD.

If a leading line is desired it is the right extreme of Golden Hill Fort 118° in line with Brambles Chine. The latter is on the middle of the coast of Colwell Bay and the fort (with flagstaff) is at the summit of the hill half a mile inland.

A useful lead in good weather, if wishing to take the short cut across the neck of the Shingle Bank between the North Head and the main part of the bank, is to keep Hurst Castle open its own width to the *left* of Sconce Point. This gives 3.0 m at low water *neap* tides, or 2.0 m at MLWS, but should be regarded with caution as the Shingle Banks are apt to shoal or shift and the channel is narrow. The lead, incidentally, is on the direct course from Hurst to Poole Bar buoy.

**From the East**

The entrance to the Solent from the east is locally known as coming in 'Through the Forts'. This means passing between No Man's Land Fort (*Fl 5s*) and Horse Sand Fort (*Fl 10s*), two large isolated structures which show clearly for many miles in good daylight visibility.

When approaching from the south or south east care must be taken to avoid Bembridge Ledge, a rocky outcrop which lies at the eastern extremity of the Isle of Wight. In poor visibility beware of mistaking the Princessa Shoal West Cardinal buoy (*Q (9) 15s*) for the Bembridge Ledge East Cardinal buoy (*Q Fl (3) 10s*). A look at the chart will convey the danger of incorrect identification.

The Nab Tower is the sentinel of this eastern approach and stands like a leaning gasholder in the middle of the ocean. It is lit (*Fl (2) 10s*) and from there to the Forts there is little to endanger the pleasure yacht, although as this is the main entrance for commercial and naval vessels using Southampton and Portsmouth a keen lookout must be kept for shipping.

When approaching from the east an area of rocks and shoals off Selsey Bill, known as the Owers, is often dangerous. The Owers LANBY (*Fl (3) 20s 22M*) marks the southern tip of this area, but there is also a short cut known as the Looe Channel only to be advised in good visibility in calm conditions.

The sandbanks and shallows at the entrances to Langstone and Chichester Harbours are described on pages 107 and 119 respectively.

Although there are passages inside both No Man's Land Fort and Horse Sand Fort these are best left to experienced Solent sailors, and first approaches into the Solent should leave No Man's Land Fort to the south and Horse Sand Fort to the north.

# 1 Keyhaven Lake and Anchorages

**Double High Water:** At Hurst, Springs −1 h 10 m, and +0 h 45 m Portsmouth. Neaps mean −0 h 5 m.
**Tidal Heights above datum:** (at Hurst) MHWS 2.7 m MLWS 0.5 m MHWN 2.3 m MLWN 1.3 m.
**Stream sets** outside off Hurst to the westward about −1 h 10 m Portsmouth, and eastward +4 h 45 m.
**Depths above datum:** Bar practically dries out. Over 3.6 m off the Camber, gradually decreasing to 1.5 m off Mount Lake and to 0.2 m off the quay.
**Yacht Clubs:** Keyhaven Yacht Club, Hurst Castle Sailing Club.

KEYHAVEN, ON THE mainland shore, is the most westerly of the Solent creeks. It lies behind Hurst Castle, which dominates the narrows of the Needles Channel. Before being taken to the scaffold, King Charles I was imprisoned here in a grim dungeon in the old round castle, but the rest of the building dates only from Victorian times and consists of flat masonry relieved by the red low and the white high lighthouses.

From Hurst to the mainland there is a mile of narrow beach which provides a natural breakwater against the prevailing winds to protect the entrance and 'Lake', or creek, which winds its way through the marram grass-covered marshes to Keyhaven. This peaceful harbour has changed little, apart from the greatly increased membership of the clubs and the demand for every possible mooring site. It is a friendly centre for small cruising yachts and keen sailors.

## Approach, Entrance and Channel

Once round the 'Trap' and Hurst Point it is possible to sail NE close inshore as far as the High Lighthouse and the old pier. Here the tidal streams vary and there is an eddy close inshore. Northward of the pier the shore is more shelving and shallow water extends seawards for a considerable distance off the cottages, and develops into a wide bar across the entrance to the river. The approach is sheltered from SW through west to north, but exposed to the east, and strangers should not attempt entry in strong winds from this direction.

Make good a position about a quarter of a mile NE of Hurst High Light when the leading marks will be seen. These consist of a front (lower) post, and a rear (higher) post both of which carry crosses (see photograph on page 16). They are situated well up on the flats. Their position is altered from time to time to suit changes in the course of the channel, but in 1991 gave a transit of 283°T. Bring the marks into line and steer on their transit. The bar nearly dries out at chart datum but about 0.6 m can be expected at MLWS and there is said to be over 1.2 m at MLWN.

The feature of the entry to the river is the North Point of the sand and shingle

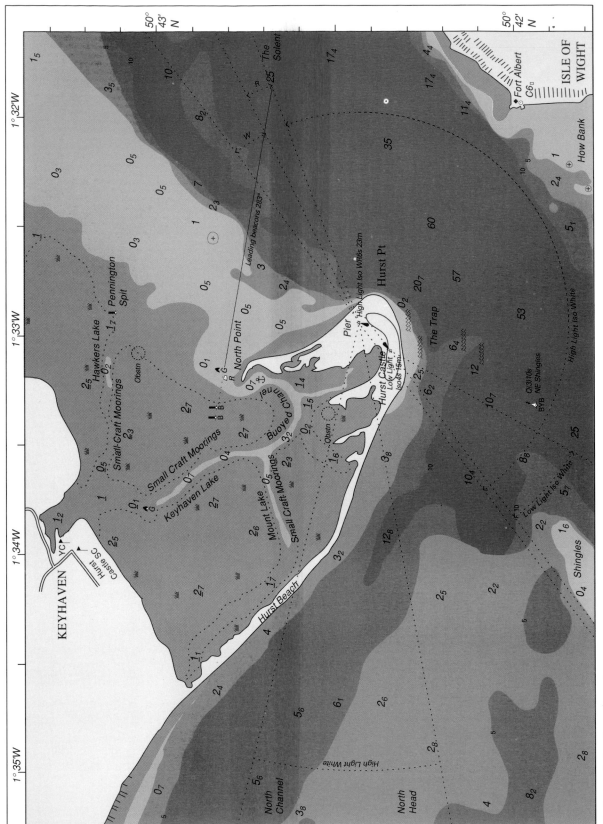

Keyhaven Lake: Soundings in metres.

Low Light    Round Fort                                    High Light

1.1.    Hurst Castle from the south-east. 'The Trap' extends approximately half a mile south from
the round fort, almost directly towards the camera.

promontory extending in a NNW direction for nearly half a mile from Hurst Point, not to
be confused with the long Hurst Beach to Milford-on-Sea. The river entrance has recently
been widened and the deepest water when rounding North Point is now in the centre of the
channel and boats of any draught should not venture too close to the point.

Continue on the transit of the leading marks until a pair of buoys R and G are seen
marking the entrance. The channel is then clearly indicated by G starboard hand buoys.
Steer to pass about 9 m off the extremity of North Point leaving another green buoy to
starboard. This is the narrowest part of the channel and there is only about 15 m between
the point and the buoy. Follow the shingle point round (once round it the channel quickly
deepens to over 3.6 m) leaving a further green buoy to starboard. The channel then leads
about WSW and the stream, which may be strong off the point, weakens.

Approaching from the eastward it is merely necessary to keep in sufficient depth of
water, steering for the High Light and pier, until on the transit of the leading marks, then
proceed as before. The stream along the Hampshire coast is much weaker inshore where it
pays to cheat a foul tide, but give the sewer outfall beacons a berth of a quarter of a mile at
low water, and note that there is an obstruction and shoal SE of the entrance to Hawker's
Lake.

After entering Keyhaven Lake at North Point a misleadingly wide expanse of water will
be seen ahead if it is near high water. The lake on the port hand is the Camber, but at low

1.2.    The anchorage east of Hurst Castle.

tide most of this dries out leaving only a short creek leading to a dilapidated private landing stage and a longer creek marked by three black and white perches beyond it, 0.6 m at LW Neaps, which winds its way through the mud to a quay near Hurst Castle. Likewise there will be a camber seen ahead north of Rabbit Point, leading westerly to Hurst beach, but this also dries out.

The picture at low water would be very different as the navigable river is then comparatively narrow. It bends round a semi-circle of gently sloping mud bank (much of which is covered at HW) from SW through west and NW almost to north. The bend in the channel is well marked by three more green buoys on the starboard side. The channel is at least 2.1 m deep as far as Mount Lake and is marked by starboard hand buoys. Above Mount Lake the river narrows and the depth falls to 1.5 m and 1.2 m for about a quarter of a mile and then to 0.9 m before the last reach, which practically dries out. The line of moorings in the **centre** of the river shows the direction of the channel very clearly, but **if the wind is blowing the yachts broadside across the fairway, steer across their bows** rather than under their sterns which may be close to the mud. In the upper reach there are three lines of small craft and the best water is close to the port hand line leaving the other two lines to starboard. When the old quay is abeam, keep to port close to the stakes which remain from an ancient quay and inside a line of fishing craft.

1.3.  The leading marks at the entrance to Keyhaven River.    1.4.  The pair of buoys at the entrance to Keyhaven River.

Mount Lake has 1.2 m at CD for over a cable from its entrance and is navigable for most of its length with sufficient rise of tide, but strangers may not find the best water as in the channel this is only about 12 m wide.

**Lights:** Keyhaven Lake has no lights, but entrance is possible if it is not too dark to identify North Point and craft moored in the river.

### Moorings, Anchorage and Facilities

Moorings are laid almost everywhere from the Camber to Keyhaven and in Mount Lake. Even in Hawker's Lake there are moorings for shallow draught yachts which can dry out. Moorings should not be picked up without local advice as the owners usually return in the evenings. The only permitted position for anchoring is in the pool immediately behind North Point, where the water is deep but there is room only for a few yachts. The position can be uncomfortable in strong SW winds and it is best to moor with two anchors which should be buoyed. Telegraph cables cross the river twice at the bend between the Camber and Mount Lake and are also laid on the river bed farther up.

There is anchorage outside off the mud flats in NW winds but the popular one is under the lee of the shingle bank between the old pier near the High Light and the cottages just north of it, where the water begins to shoal and anchorage is necessarily farther out. The anchorage is sheltered from SW, W and NW winds but suffers from the swell of passing ships. It is used principally in day time when as many as twenty or more yachts bring up on a summer afternoon, and use dinghies to land on the shingle or to proceed up the river to Keyhaven. During gales the anchorage is uncomfortable owing to tidal eddies but it provides tolerable shelter in good holding ground and may be useful if arriving at night when the tide is turning foul in the Solent.

At Keyhaven there is a poor public landing on steps at the end of the old quay (scheduled for replacement in 1992) and a new quay beyond the yacht clubs with dinghy landing at the hard adjacent to it. Both quays dry almost completely at low tide and are not suitable for overnight stops. The River Warden (Mr Tom Holt) has an office between the Keyhaven Yacht Club and the new quay. Near the Keyhaven Yacht Club (with its private dinghy pontoon) and the Hurst Castle Sailing Club, there is the yacht yard of the West Solent Boat Builders who undertake laying-up and repairs and provide fuel and water for yachts. At the hard, where there is 1.8 m at HW Springs, yachts can be scrubbed, and there is a launching site for dinghies, though it is often congested in the season, particularly at week-ends. Behind the Keyhaven Yacht Club there is a car park and the Gun Inn is just across the road. Buses very occasionally run to Milford-on-Sea, a mile distant, where there are the usual facilities of a small town (EC Wednesday). In summer there are motor launches from the quay to Hurst Castle which is open to the public.

During 1992 the National Rivers Authority will be rebuilding the harbour wall at Keyhaven, inevitably causing major disruption around the quay, yacht club, sailing club and boatyard. These areas are already congested at weekends and space will be at a particular premium while work is taking place. Visitors are advised to remain downstream in the anchorage and come up to the quay by dinghy.

1.5. The River Warden's office and the hard at the new quay.

1.6.    View from the hard at low water showing the channel between the fishing craft and the wall.

## Alum Bay

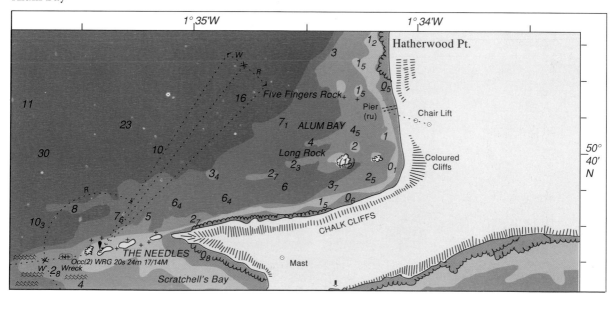

**Nearby Anchorages**

Yarmouth Roads is the nearest anchorage to Hurst Road – see Yarmouth – but there are two interesting ones in the Needles Channel. The nearest is Totland Bay (distance only 1.5 miles from Hurst) which is sheltered in southerly and easterly winds. If draught allows, anchor close inshore between the pier and the old life-boat house, where there is good holding ground in sand and mud. Further out there is a heavy growth of weed and holding is less sure. There is a light at the pier head (*2F G vert*).

Alum Bay, over a mile farther towards the Needles, is famous for its multi-coloured cliffs at the foot of which there are sands suitable for children. There is a cliff path and chair-lift leading to large motor coach and car parks, and a café. Nowadays there may be many yachts in the bay on a summer's day. The anchorage is good in southerly and easterly winds, though during gales squalls come down from the cliffs above. If sheltering in a southerly gale be prepared to leave quickly in the event of the wind veering later towards NW, as this may put the yacht on a lee shore. The anchorage is little used at night but the Shingles buoys are an aid to navigation. The best position is off the ruins of the pier, of which only one pile and an inner pair remain standing. Less than 150 m to the northward of the approach is the Five Finger Rock 0.6 m CD, and to the southward the Long Rock. Long Rock is in two parts, the inshore section of which dries out about 0.6 m CD and is often marked by a lobster-pot buoy. The westerly section is awash at CD and difficult to spot. Together they are a danger to craft leaving an inshore anchorage and proceeding direct to the Needles. Both Five Fingers and Long Rock can be avoided by keeping Warren Fort open to Hatherwood Point until what is left of the ruined pier bears east before sailing in to the required depth of water. Those familiar with Alum Bay may pass between the ledges off Hatherwood Point and Fiver Fingers Rock.

1.7.  The old life-boat house at Totland Bay.

# 2 Yarmouth Harbour

**Double High Water:** Springs − 1 h 5 m and + 0 h 50 m. Portsmouth. Neaps mean + 0 h 5 m.
**Tidal Heights above datum:** MHWS 3.1 m MLWS 0.6 m MHWN 2.5 m MLWN 1.4 m.
**Stream sets** outside strongly to the westward − 1 h 15 m Portsmouth and to the eastward + 4 h 50 m.
**Depths above datum:** 2.1 m in the approach channel and about 1.8 m in the harbour itself.
**Yacht Clubs:** Royal Solent Yacht Club, Yarmouth Sailing club.

YARMOUTH IS UNDOUBTEDLY the most popular of the Solent harbours for visiting yachts, being at a convenient distance from most centres in the Solent and providing good deep water berths. The harbour is very well run for yachtsmen and provides the best port of departure if bound west or to France.

The town itself has a mellow charm and the castle at the harbour entrance lends a medieval appearance as viewed from the sea.

In the Middle Ages Yarmouth and its harbour provided the first objective for attack by any French squadrons entering the Solent. It was not until the castle was built for its defence in 1537 that the town really began to prosper and grow. This massive building still remains in good condition and is preserved as an ancient monument. Behind the castle stands what was once the house of the Governor of the Island, where Charles II made a short stay while on a visit to Hurst. It is now the George Hotel, much frequented by yachtsmen.

At high water a dinghy can proceed up the River Yar and along the winding creek nearly to Freshwater. The surrounding woods, the reeds and pools backed by hills make this a pleasant trip. There are coastal walks from Yarmouth in the direction of the Needles and eastwards to Newtown.

## The Approach and Entrance

Approaching from the west there are two things to consider. In deep water by the Black Rock buoy some three-quarters of a mile to the west of the entrance there is Fiddler's Race, a genuine small scale race, which can be dangerous for dinghies and unpleasant for yachts of small size. Farther inshore lies the rock itself which dries 0.6 m at low tide. Small craft can pass inside the rock, thus avoiding the race, by keeping the end of Victoria Pier, 90 m east of Sconce Point in line with Hurst Castle. This course is said to allow 0.6 m at MLWS, but almost dries out at chart datum.

The approach from the east is easy, and it is only necessary to make allowance for the

2.1.   The entrance to Yarmouth.

strong tidal streams and at night to avoid the row of large mooring buoys, three of which are unlit. By keeping on a course a little outside the end of the pier there is ample water for any yacht. Small craft can keep farther inshore to cheat the tide, except at low water when there is very little depth inside the pier end on the east side.

Make a position about 50 m west of the end of Yarmouth Pier and bring the leading marks (black and white diamonds on posts set behind the quay) into line at 187°. Steer on or close to this transit, but avoid being set too far eastward of it by wind or tide or when tacking. The channel narrows as the entrance is approached but carries 2.1 m as far as the ferry jetty and 1.8 m beyond it. Course should be altered to leave the jetty and ramp to port. Ferries run regular services across the Solent to Lymington and, when approaching and entering Yarmouth, visitors must keep clear of these large and unmanoeuvrable vessels. The speed limit in the harbour is 4 knots.

When the ferry ramp comes abeam to port, the main channel turns to the west parallel with the inside of the breakwater, leaving the A line of mooring piles for larger yachts to starboard and the B line to port. In addition, there are three lines of mooring piles for smaller yachts with narrow fairways between them. Incoming yachts should have warps and fenders ready and are usually hailed from a boat by one of the Berthing Masters giving berthing instructions. If the Berthing Master or his Deputy is not immediately available it is best to berth temporarily at the Town Quay and await directions, as anchoring is

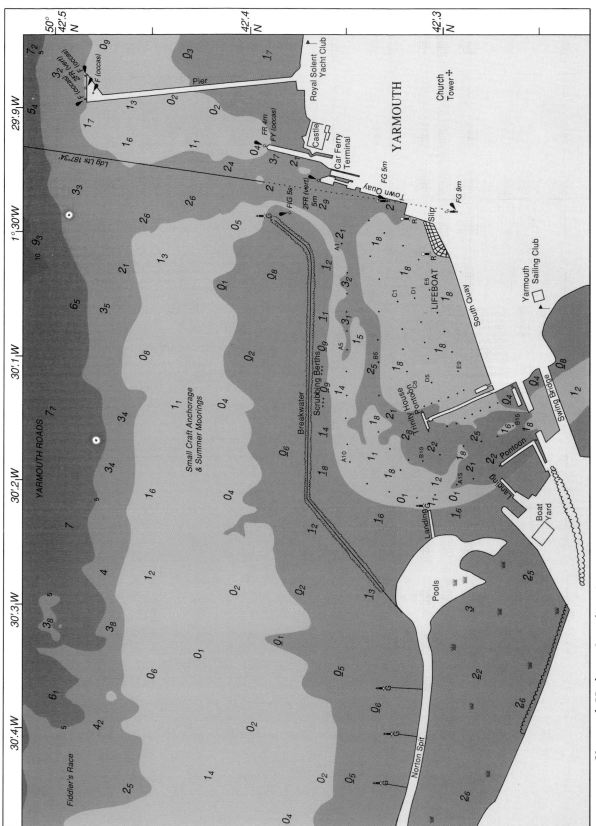

**Yarmouth Harbour:** Soundings in metres.

2.2.   The temporary berths at Town Quay.

prohibited. No official VHF watch is maintained by the Harbour Master or Berthing Masters.

Within the harbour there is not a great range of tide, only about 2.4 m on ordinary spring tides, but the stream can be quite strong, especially on the ebb. There is no room for tacking in the narrow fairway, especially if other craft or dinghies are under way. Auxiliary power must be used. Depths vary within the harbour, which tends to silt but is dredged during the winter. It is best to regard the whole harbour as about 1.8 m. There are two tide gauges, one on pile A1 and the other on the Town Quay.

**Entry Prohibited:** When the harbour is full red flags are hoisted both at the Pier Head and on a flagpole at the seaward end of the ferry jetty, and a 'HARBOUR FULL' sign displayed which is illuminated at night. Yarmouth is so popular that the harbour can be full by early afternoon on Saturdays in summer although, in the event of a yacht leaving, the Harbour Master may authorize a yacht to enter and occupy the vacant berth.

**Lights:** There are two fixed green lights on the leading marks. The end of the pier outside the harbour is marked by two fixed red vertical lights and in fog two white lights are shown. The end of the ferry jetty is also marked by two fixed red vertical lights and in fog a fixed yellow light. The dolphin on the starboard side of the entrance is marked by a flashing green light, and the car ferry terminal inner jetty by a further pair of fixed red vertical lights.

2.3.    South Quay on the left with the fuelling station and the lifeboat on its exclusive mooring.

## Moorings, Anchorages and Facilities

The harbour comes under the authority of the Yarmouth Harbour Commissioners, whose powers were widened under an Act of Parliament to include the approach, the pier and water adjacent to it, and also the River Yar above the bridge.

Yarmouth is a natural yacht harbour but the dredging in 1958, and the South Quay which followed, enclosed some 70 acres accommodating about 300 yachts, and more at times. The development was an example of enterprise long before the creation of any marinas in this country. Dredging and improvements have continued and the harbour is a model for good relations between the controlling authority and the yachtsmen using it. Harbour dues are reasonable.

Yachts berth fore and aft to the piles of which there are five lines, A, B, C, D and E. The piles on each line are numbered from the entrance. The berth between No 5 and 6 E piles is allotted to the lifeboat. Care must be taken always to moor to the piles and not to other yachts, apart from breast ropes or temporarily on arrival or departure.

When the harbour is full, anchorage may be found outside, to the west of the pierhead clear of the entrance channel and south of the big ship moorings. This anchorage is reasonable in offshore winds or in settled weather, though the holding is not good. Tidal streams are strong so it is best to anchor as close inshore as safety permits. The anchorage is exposed to all northerly winds and it is said that in the gale of 1876 a ketch of 1.8 m

2.4.   Looking up the River Yar from the swing bridge.

draught, anchored in the roads, was swept by huge seas right over the breakwater, which presumably was then lower than it is today. In northerly gales and on a big spring tide even the harbour itself can be uncomfortable near high water. During the summer months visitors' moorings are laid in this area. A fee is payable, and dues will be collected by the Berthing Master.

If a prolonged stay is intended, the Harbour Master should be consulted. He is Mr N. G. Ward, and has an office near the Town Quay (Tel: 0983 760321). The duty Berthing Master may be found at the Harbour Office on South Quay (Tel: as above).

Landing in Yarmouth Harbour is easy as there are several slips and pontoons. There is a 5-ton crane, fuel pumps, water, a marine engineer's workshop (where batteries can be charged), slipway and dinghy compound at the South Quay, which extends the whole length of the bridge road between the training groyne and the town. Yachts may go alongside for petrol (available for DIY use) water, bottled gas, etc. Although periodically dredged to 2.4 m, silting inevitably occurs and it is safer to take it as 1.8 m. There are two scrubbing berths on piles near the breakwater for yachts up to 1.8 m draught on application to the Harbour Master.

The town of Yarmouth itself is well adapted to the needs of yachtsmen. The Royal Solent YC is a leading and hospitable yacht club and the Yarmouth SC has been re-established; two hotels (the George and the Bugle), the Wheatsheaf and other inns and small restaurants add to the facilities. Customs formalities are quick as their office (Quay Street) is open from 0600 to 2200 in summer months. The PO is in Quay St, next to a booksellers, stationers and newsagents (including Sunday papers), and there are small shops of all kinds, EC Wednesday. There are three yacht yards: Harold Hayles (Yarmouth IW) Ltd, just west of the bridge, and above the bridge the River Yar Boat Yard which lays up many yachts. Launching sites from dinghy slips at the quays or from the ferry slip by arrangement with Harbour Master. Car park adjacent. The lifeboat is famous for her work in the Needles Channel and south of the Island. Frequent ferries run to Lymington and in the summer there are occasional excursion steamers to Bournemouth and elsewhere. Sandhard Ferries provide a useful local service to the bathing beach and to yachts. There are good bus connections.

It is possible for a shallow draft yacht with mast in situ to proceed above the new swing bridge around HW. Enquire at the Harbour Master's office for bridge opening times.

2.5.   Looking WSW from near the harbour entrance.

# 3 Lymington River

**Double High Water:** Springs −0 h 55 m and +0 h 45 m Portsmouth; Neaps mean +0 h 5 m.
**Tidal Heights above datum:** MHWS 3.0 m MLWS 0.45 m MHWN 2.6 m MLWN 1.3 m.
**Stream sets** to the westward off Lymington Spit about −1 h 15 m Portsmouth, and eastward +4 h 50 m.
**Depths:** There is a minimum depth of 1.8 m in mid-channel from the river entrance to the pier railway station and Berthon Boat Co Ltd, gradually shoaling towards the channel margins. From the Berthon to the Town Quay and bridge there is a least depth of 1.1 m. The width of the channel above Harper's Post is restored by dredging from time to time.
**Yacht Clubs:** Royal Lymington Yacht Club, Lymington Town Sailing Club.

THE CHANNEL WINDS its way through marshes to Lymington, the old world town whose history from far into the past has been associated with ships and the sea. At one time it was an important local centre of salt and iron-smelting industries, the ironstone being quarried at Hengistbury and brought to Lymington by sea in barges and beaten out by great hammers worked by water wheel from the 'hammer ponds', of which Sowley is one. 'Jack in the Basket', the beacon with a barrel top in the approach to Lymington, used to be taken as a point of departure for ships, and it was from here that HMS *Pandora* sailed in 1790 to search the Pacific for the mutineers from the *Bounty*.

Today the river is little used for commercial purposes other than by the car ferries to Yarmouth, but it has grown to be an important yachting centre with two of the leading marinas in the Solent and many river moorings. The river is deep enough for most yachts except very deep craft at extreme LW springs and the yachting facilities are excellent. The town itself has grown but it retains its character and much of its old-world charm.

### The Approach, Entrance and River

When entering the river the best water will be found by leaving Jack in the Basket about 50 m to port to clear Cross Boom (next port hand pile) by approximately 40 m to port. Thereafter the river is well marked by red piles with can-type topmarks on the port hand and by green piles with green triangular topmarks to starboard. The deepest part of the fairway in cross-section is about in the middle third as the channel tends to shoal towards the sides. The beacons should be given a wide berth as many of them are on the mud or in very shallow water. The line of yachts on moorings near the mud on the west side of the river provide an additional aid to pilotage. Two leading posts, with red and white horizontal stripes, are erected on the flats to the south of Seymours Post to provide a transit for the outgoing ferries and another pair, with black and white horizontal stripes, on the flats on the east side of the river south of the Cage Boom for the incoming ferry transit.

The car ferries are the only features disconcerting to the stranger. These are handled with care but are big for the river and should not be passed too closely, especially by dinghies, owing to the suction they cause in the restricted water. The ferries have right of way and

3.1.   The entrance with Jack in the Basket extreme left and the Royal Lymington YC starting platform on the right.

3.2.   Long Reach with No. 2 port hand beacon, (Cross Boom), on the left.

3.3.   The starboard turn around Tar Barrel.

3.4.   The two black and white transit beacons are to the right of the ferry.

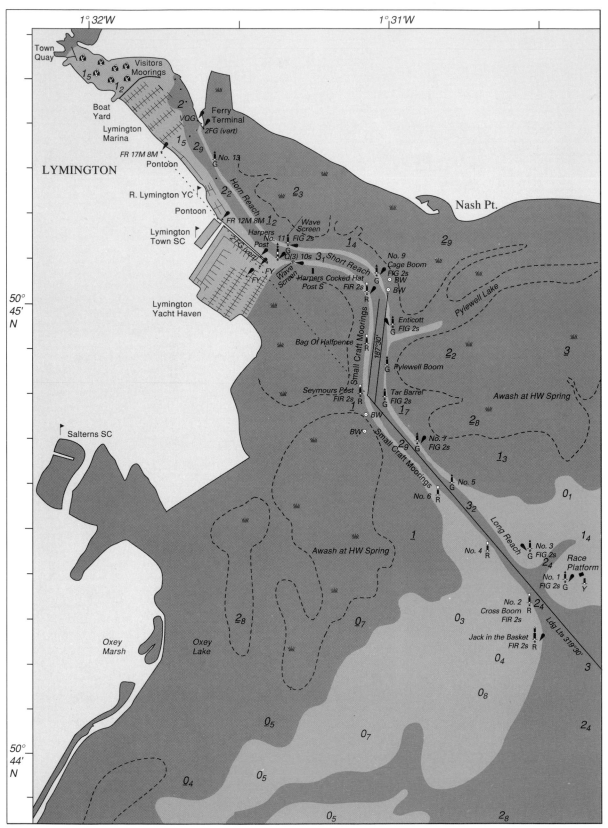

Town Quay

1₅

Visitors Moorings

1₂

Boat Yard

2·

Lymington Marina

VQG

Ferry Terminal

2FG (vert)

1₅

FR 17M 8M

Pontoon

2₉

No. 13

G

LYMINGTON

R. Lymington YC

2₂

Horn Reach

2₃

Pontoon

FR 12M 8M

1₂

Wave Screen

Harpers Post

FlG 2s

No. 11

1₄

Lymington Town SC

2FG (vert)

G

Q(3) 10s

3₁

Short Reach

No. 9 Cage Boom

2₉

Nash Pt.

FlG 2s

FY

Wave Screen

Harpers Cocked Hat

FlR 2s

G

BW

BW

FY

Post S

R

Pylewell Lake

Enticott

FlG 2s

Lymington Yacht Haven

50° 45' N

Bag Of Halfpence

Small Craft Moorings

187°30'

2₂

3

G

Pylewell Boom

Tar Barrel

FlG 2s

Seymours Post

FlR 2s

1

1₇

2₈

Salterns SC

BW

BW

2₉

No. 7

FlG 2s

G

Awash at HW Spring

Small Craft Moorings

No. 5

1₃

G

No. 6

R

3₂

0₁

Long Reach

1

Awash at HW Spring

No. 4

R

No. 3

FlG 2s

G

1₄

2₄

Race Platform

No. 1

FlG 2s

G

Y

2₄

2₈

Oxey Lake

0₇

No. 2 Cross Boom

FlR 2s

0₃

Ldg Lts 319°30'

Oxey Marsh

Jack in the Basket

FlR 2s

R

0₄

3

0₅

0₈

0₅

0₇

2₄

0₄

0₅

0₅

2₈

**Lymington River:** Soundings in metres.

3.5.   Short Reach. The wave screens extending from the channel to the left and right.

3.6.   Harper's Post South on the left. The entrance to Lymington Yacht Haven lies beyond it and the wave screen, leaving Harpers Post, just to the right of the crane, to starboard.

3.7.   Horn Reach with the Royal Lymington YC. The main channel continues on the right of the picture.

3.8.    Above the ferry terminal the river becomes congested and can be tricky to follow. Here the main channel lies between the (red) midstream pile and the ferry pier to starboard.

can be quite a problem at low water if several yachts are in the vicinity at the same time. There is a speed limit of 6 knots in the river.

Wavescreens have recently been constructed on either side of the channel at the western end of Short Reach, in order to reduce fetch and improve protection for the moorings upriver of the Yacht Haven entrance. They take the form of piled wooden barrages standing 4 m above CD. The wavescreen to the north of the fairway extends from a position 9 m north of No 11 Post for 100 m in a north-easterly direction. It is unlit. That to the south commences about 82 m north-west of Harper's Post South and extends 80 m in a south-westerly direction. It is lit by two fixed red vertical lights at the channel end. Great care must be taken to avoid these obstructions, particularly at night.

Horn Reach is the last reach up to the pier railway station and the narrowest. Harper's Post, now an east cardinal mark, indicates the spit of mud that divides the entrance to the Lymington Yacht Haven from Horn Reach, which leads between moored boats past the public pontoon, the launching slip and the Royal Lymington Yacht Club's pontoon. Beyond these, also on the port hand, lies the Lymington Marina, the main channel leading between the red piles in midstream and the pier ferry terminal. The channel then bends round the end of the marina, leaving a large mooring area to starboard, and turns to the west towards the Berthon Boat Co Ltd. This part of the channel above the ferry terminal is slightly narrower due principally to the craft moored on piles on either side. Subject to silting it carries 1.8 m as far as the yacht yard and is dredged to 1.4 m to the north end of the visitors' pontoon at the Town Quay. Fishing boats and shallow draft yachts lie on moorings beyond the Quay, but depths shoal swiftly.

**Lights:** There are two fixed red lights which lead up Long Reach at 320° as far as Seymore's Post. The river is marked on the port side by *Fl R* lights and Harper's Post *Q (3) 10s*. On the starboard hand there are *Fl G* lights.

### Moorings, Anchorage and Facilities

Anchorage is prohibited in the river, which is fully occupied by moorings controlled by the Harbour Commissioners and rented annually, but anchorage can be found outside off the mud flats in offshore winds. Both marinas are mainly occupied by permanently berthed yachts, but visitors can usually be accommodated temporarily, preferably by telephoning in advance.

The Harbour Master, Mr F. V. Woodfort (Tel: 0590 672014), has his office in a three-storey building between the Royal Lymington YC and the Lymington Town SC, with the customs office above. He will advise on use of the visitor's pontoon at the Town Quay (maximum 40 ft LOA) and the adjacent buoys. An enlarged area to the south-east of the Town Quay has recently been dredged and there are large white buoys with metal rings to which visiting yachts (about 35 ft LOA) can moor bow and stern. This area is congested on summer weekends and visitors can expect to secure several yachts abreast on the buoys and up to six abreast alongside. Altogether there are now berths for about 150 visiting yachts, in addition to the marinas. Dues are collected daily. Yachts up to 1.8 m draught may be scrubbed at the Town Slip, booked through the Harbour Master. Car park, water and public lavatories are adjacent and also the Ship Hotel, chandlers and nearby in Quay Hill good shops for yachting clothes and oilskins.

The largest yacht yard is the Berthon Boat Co Ltd, just north of their marina, which has craftsmen for all kinds of repairs and yacht building, including ocean racers. The Lymington Yacht Haven has an extensive chandlery nearby. The town offers every facility for yacht repair and maintenance and is the home of many famous names in yachting such as Brookes and Gatehouse, Hood Sailmakers and Laurent Giles Ltd.

Water can be had at the marina pontoons, the Town Quay and the public pontoon and fuel at the marinas. There are dinghy launching sites at slipways adjacent to the yacht clubs and Town Quay.

The main shopping centre is in the High Street which, despite the addition of a few multiple shops, has changed little over the centuries, and leads up the hill from Quay Street to St Thomas' Church. Here will be found banks and good individual shops of every description including a leading bookshop. EC Wednesday. A busy street market operates every Saturday. There are several hotels, restaurants and garages and travel agents. Communications are excellent: from pier and town stations to Brockenhurst linking up with fast electric trains (Waterloo, Southampton, Bournemouth and Weymouth), buses to all parts and frequent car ferries to Yarmouth, IOW. The New Forest, with its lovely countryside, is within easy reach.

# 4 Newtown River

**Double High Water:** Springs about −1 h 0 m and +0 h 50 m Portsmouth; Neaps mean −0 h 5 m.
**Tidal Heights above datum** at Solent Banks: MHWS 3.4 m MLWS 0.5 m MHWN 2.8 m MLWN 1.5 m.
**Stream sets** outside to the westward −1 h 15 m Portsmouth, and to the eastward +4 h 45 m.
**Depths:** About 0.9 m on the bar; 1.5 m to 3.3 m in channel as far as Fishhouse Pt 1.2 m with deeper pools within, falling to 0.9 m at junction with Causeway Lake and shallow beyond.

THERE MUST BE few yachtsmen who, after visiting Newtown for the first time, have not returned to it again year after year. The snug anchorage, the creeks winding silently through the marshes and the unspoilt countryside, combine to give the place a character of its own. Perhaps the finger-prints of history linger on in some distant way to the present time.

Newtown, under its original name of Francheville, was once the capital of the Isle of Wight and a flourishing seaport. In 1377 the town was sacked and burnt by the French. When partially rebuilt, the name was changed to Newtown, but it was too vulnerable to attack from the sea for its former prosperity to be regained. However, from 1585 to 1832 it returned two Members of Parliament, which included John Churchill, later Duke of Marlborough. The Old Town Hall has been skilfully restored and maintained in perfect repair by the National Trust, and is well worth visiting. There are still lanes and cuttings through the trees that once were busy streets some 600 years ago.

The village now consists only of a church and a few houses and cottages. There are no ships in the river but many yachts, so many in fact that it is preferable if possible to avoid a visit on August week-ends and bank holidays.

## The Approaches and Creeks

Newtown River lies on the Island shore, 3½ miles east of Yarmouth and nearly a mile ESE of Hamstead Ledge. The best time for a first visit is on a rising tide before the mud flats are covered and the trend of the channels can still be seen. At high water everything is covered and strangers often go aground despite the perches marking the mud.

Approaching from the west make Hamstead Ledge green conical buoy. Here the stream is very strong and the water rough if the wind is contrary to it. In good weather the buoy can be passed on the wrong side, leaving it no more than half a mile to port and crossing the ledges in over 6 m. Then steer due east for half a mile, when the small red spherical bar buoy will be close at hand.

Leading Marks          Fishhouse Pt.

4.1.  Newtown entrance from seaward. The leading marks are indicated and should be lined up on 130° when south of the bar buoy. The other two posts have been removed since the photo was taken.

4.2.  The leading marks at low water. Fishhouse Point is on the extreme right. Best water will be found on the western side of the channel.

4.3.    The river entrance with Fishhouse Point on the left. The yacht aground in the centre indicates
the shingle bank which dries out. It is marked by green perches, sometimes weathered, but, as
can be seen, these should be given a wide berth. This picture was taken at MLWS with an
easterly wind and a low run of tide.

From the eastward, keep Yarmouth Pier well open of Hamstead Point to avoid Newtown
Gravel Banks and leave the bar buoy to port. The entrance to the river and the leading
marks will then be seen. The entrance lies between two shingle spits, at the east end of the
shingle shore extending for half a mile east of Hamstead Point, which is backed by a line of
low trees for most of the distance. The leading marks consist of two beacon posts on the
mud to the east of the entrance on the north side of Fishhouse Point. The outer one is
painted with RW stripes and has a Y topmark and the inner bears a white disc within a
black circle.

Best water will be found by keeping the spherical red bar buoy close to port and lining up
the leading beacons on 130° when almost due south of the buoy. This transit leads close
past a spherical green starboard hand buoy which marks a steep gravel bank on the west
side. Abandon the transits just before this buoy comes abeam to steer directly for the centre
of the entrance. Depths shoal rapidly to the east and a closer approach to the outer leading
beacon may result in grounding.

The channel is subject to periodic fluctuations in both depth and direction. It currently
carries a minimum of 2 m from the bar buoy to the narrows, where it deepens to over 5 m
before shoaling to around 2 m off Lower Hamstead Quay.

Just inside the entrance two drying shingle banks lie on the starboard side of the channel.
Despite their being clearly marked by green perches with triangular green topmarks,
strangers often run aground here by steering direct towards yachts at anchor or on
moorings and leaving the perches on the wrong side. As will be seen from the chart, after
the entrance has been passed there is a pronounced bend in the river. It then runs SE
towards a red port hand perch with a red can topmark, on the north side of the entrance of

Clamerkin Lake, before bending round to the SSW where a number of yachts on moorings lie in the centre of the channel. Note that on the south side of the entrance to Clamerkin Lake there is a green perch, which is a starboard mark when entering this channel but must be left to port when continuing up Newtown River. The channel is then easiest to follow by keeping close to the yachts on moorings as the deep water is very narrow. Near the junction with Causeway Lake the depth falls to about half a mile. Beyond this the water quickly shoals. At low tide there is little water in the upper tributaries, namely Western Haven and Shalfleet Lake: in fact, at low spring tides Shalfleet Lake dries out, although it is navigable at low water neap tides in a dinghy. The main arm of the harbour is only marked as far as the junction with Causeway Lake.

Clamerkin Lake is fairly deep, having over 1.2 m of water at CD for a considerable distance, but care must be taken in the lower reaches as the channel is gradually changing its course to the north-west. The channel is marked by occasional perches but the line of yachts at anchor and on moorings assists pilotage. There is danger from rifle practice at the top of the creek and in Spur Lake; red flags are flown during firing.

4.4.   Looking up Newtown River. The yachts on moorings indicate the trend of the channel. The Lower Hamstead landing is about a quarter of a mile up on the starboard side.

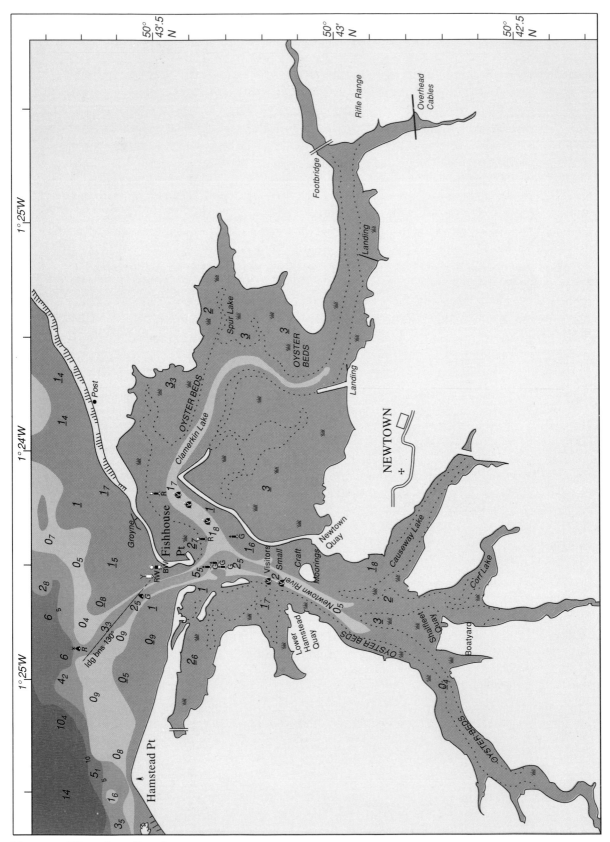

**Newtown River:** Soundings in metres.

**Lights:** None in the river.

### Moorings, Anchorage and Facilities

There is a good temporary anchorage during offshore winds outside the entrance in the vicinity of Hamstead Point, or elsewhere as depth permits. This is now much used if the river itself is crowded. The best anchorage in the river is in the first reach of the channel between the entrance and the permanent moorings belonging to local yachts – see below for the possibility of hiring one – or in the lower part of Clamerkin Lake. In strong northerly winds the entrance and anchorage can be rough near high water, especially on the first of the ebb at springs when the stream is strong. Better shelter is found farther up the river near the junction with Causeway Lake in about 0.9 m at CD plus 0.5 m at MLWS or 1.5 m at MLWN, but the best positions are now occupied by permanent moorings. Centreboard or very light draught yachts, however, may be able to find snug anchorage beyond the permanent moorings.

Yachts are not permitted to anchor beyond the anchorage limits marked by notice boards, owing to the proximity of oyster beds in Clamerkin Lake and Newtown River. Anchors should be buoyed when anchoring near permanent moorings, which are connected by ground chains.

There are three visitors' moorings (conspicuous white buoys) in Clamerkin Lake and more white buoys in the main arm leading to Shalfleet. Application should be made to the Harbour Master (Mr K. B. Abernethy, Tel: 0983 78424). He or his Deputy may be found at the black shed near Newtown Quay. They visit yachts to collect harbour dues, which are payable for mooring or anchorage. They are well earned, for without the River Committee there would, at times, be absolute chaos owing to too many yachts in too small an area. If they are not collected it is requested that any dues will be placed in the National Trust box behind the shed. Newtown Quay and the adjoining sea walls are undergoing repair, and large barges and lighters manoeuvre in the area during spring tides.

There is a public landing on the east side of the river north of the quay. Facilities for yachts are limited, which is perhaps a good thing as the charm of the creeks lies in the lack of development of the unspoilt countryside. At Lower Hamstead on the west side of the river there is a private landing but yachtsmen are allowed to use it at their own risk. From the landing it is only 200 yards to the farm where there is a camp site and water point. Alternatively, make a dinghy excursion to the quay by the old salting in Shalfleet Lake; then follow the track along the bank of the creek to Shalfleet Village, where there is the New Inn and nearby, in Warlands Lane, a small shop and PO. The village lies on the main bus route between Yarmouth and Newport. There is a small yacht yard and slip at Shalfleet Quay and near high water the creek is navigable by shoal draught yachts. Apply at the yacht yard for a mooring, of which there are a fair number in the reach off the quay for craft of shoal draught.

4.5.    Shalfleet Quay.

The creeks provide interesting sailing for dinghy excursions and there are many splendid walks. The whole estuary and much of the surrounding land is the property of the National Trust and it is requested that the Trust's bye-laws be observed. The land and marshes near the creeks provide nesting places for countless sea and water birds. During the nesting season April–June inclusive 'No Landing' notices are placed on Fishhouse Point.

# 5 Beaulieu River

**Double High Water** at entrance: Springs −0 h 45 m Portsmouth and +1 h 20 m; Neaps mean +0 h 5 m.
**Tidal Heights above datum** at entrance approx: MHWS 3.7 m MLWS 0.6 m MHWN 3.1 m MLWN 1.6 m.
**Stream sets** to the westward off East Lepe Buoy about −1 h 0 m Portsmouth, and to the eastward about +4 h 45 m Portsmouth.
**Depths:** Bar on leading line 0.6 m CD. The river bed is uneven with from a depth of 1.5 m up to 6.0 m as far as Bucklers Hard, except for a few shoaler patches referred to below.
**Yacht Clubs:** R Southampton YC, Beaulieu River SC.

OF ALL THE Solent creeks and harbours, Beaulieu River is undoubtedly the most beautiful. From the entrance its wide channel leads west between marshes, the sanctuary of sea birds, and then takes a turn to the northward bringing the yachtsman within the 'perambulations of the Forest'.

Bucklers Hard, situated on the west bank about half way up the river was established by John, Duke of Montagu, in the eighteenth century and became the scene of shipbuilding activities. In the wide street between cottages and Bucklers Hard lay piled the Forest oak from which the wooden walls of Nelson's days were built. The house of Henry Adams, the famous shipbuilder, is still standing, and is now preserved as 'The Master Builder's House' hotel.

From Bucklers Hard the river pursues a wandering course through the Forest for two miles, drying out at low water in the last reach leading to Beaulieu. Here there is the historic abbey, believed to have been founded by King John and built by the Cistercian monks in the year 1204. The monks were given a charter with the maximum possible privileges, which tradition attributes to the consequence of the King's bad dream after he had ordered his servants to trample certain monks under the feet of their horses. In more recent times the ancient rights of the monks, confirmed by various sovereigns to the successive owners of Beaulieu, were inherited by Lord Montagu and the Trustees of the Beaulieu Estate. These rights, almost without parallel in the British Isles, include ownership of the bed of the river and foreshore, flotsam, jetsam, lagan and wreck. From the yachtsmen's point of view the landowner's rights have been an advantage. They have prevented unsightly development and, besides keeping the river unspoilt, have led to the entrance and channel being properly boomed and the appointment of a Harbour Master who is most helpful to visiting yachtsmen, besides collecting the dues.

## The Approach, Entrance and Channel
Approaching the entrance from the westward keep well off shore to avoid the shallow water off the Warren Flat and Beaulieu Spit until the conspicuous coastguard cottages, a

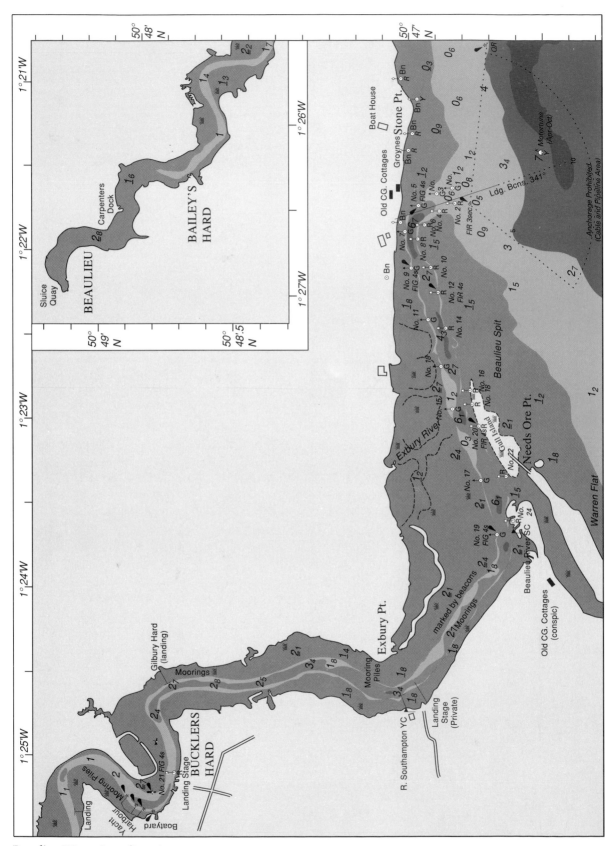

**Beaulieu River:** Soundings in metres.

white boathouse and the conspicuous tripod dolphin (which bears a light *Fl R 5s* and a notice limiting speed to 5 knots) are identified and the entrance is opened up. The dolphin marks the west side of the entrance and stands in shallow water at the eastern end of Beaulieu Spit, which covers on the last quarter of the flood. The front leading mark has an orange board with an angular top on the first port hand pile and the rear is a similar orange mark on a pole. The latter is not so clear as it is among trees situated about 200 m west of the conspicuous ex-coastguard cottages and white boathouse on the shore. They transit on 341°. However silting has taken place since these beacons were positioned, and a shoal carrying only 0.5 m at CD has formed on the leading line from 100 m to 300 m from the outer dolphin. Better water will be found by leaving the leading marks open to the east, but even so yachts routinely ground on the bar around low water. In strong onshore winds the area should be avoided from half ebb to half flood.

When approaching Beaulieu River from the eastward keep well clear of the shoals between Stansore Pt and Stone Pt, marked by three beacons (*Q R*) situated near the 5 m line. See chartlet opposite for information on cable area. Shoal water continues to extend about a quarter of a mile from the shore west of the beacons, and it is simplest after passing the most westerly beacon to bring it into line with the middle beacon and sail on this stern transit until just short of the leading line and enter as described above.

Once over the bar, depths increase to 2.1 m in the vicinity of No 1 beacon and 5 m or more by No 3 beacon. The channel is clearly marked by piles with reflectors. On the port hand these are red piles (even numbers) with can tops and red reflectors and on the starboard hand green piles (odd numbers) with green conical tops and green reflectors. Booms and perches are placed on the edge of the mud and should not be approached closely.

Steer for No 5 pile beacon (*Fl G 4s*), keeping within the port and starboard piles until you can turn to the west toward No 9 pile beacon (*Fl G 4s*). Pass No 12 beacon (*Fl R 4s*) and No 20 beacon (*Fl R 4s*) to port and you will see No 19 starboard hand beacon (*Fl G 4s*) which indicates where the river begins to bend again off the jetty of the Beaulieu River SC at Need's Ore Point. Here it turns to the NW and leads past Gin's Farm and the Royal Southampton YC. This reach is deep except in the vicinity of a shoal on the east side shown on the chart. At Gin's Farm there is a hard and a private pier. 150 m beyond this is the jetty and pontoon of the R Southampton YC, and the pile moorings reserved for the club. Here the river bends to NNE and then to N for the mile reach up to Gilbury Hard. The channel is wide and clear with more than 2 m at CD. Off Gilbury Hard it turns sharply to the westward up to Bucklers Hard, where shoals run out well beyond the eastern bank, marked by No 21 beacon (*Fl G 4s*). Above Bucklers Hard the depths vary considerably from 0.9 m to 2.7 m as far as the pier at Spearbed Copse, and the channel is navigable with sufficient rise of tide as far as the brickworks at Bailey's Hard where there is a landing. Beyond this the river dries out at CD, though it can be used by shallow draught craft near high water up to Timbrell's Quay at Beaulieu. All the jetties on the river are private, but in addition to the

5.1.  Beaulieu River entrance looking north, showing from the left the dolphin at the entrance with the light (*Fl R 5s*), the two leading marks, the back one partly hidden in the trees and the coastguard cottages on the right. The dolphin is left about 100 m to port.

5.2.  A nearer view of the leading marks.

hards mentioned, there are landings at Gilbury Hard, 200 m beyond the jetty (Exbury village and stores three-quarters of a mile walk) and at Keeping Trees, half a mile beyond Bucklers Hard.

**Moorings, Anchorage and Facilities**

Beaulieu River is one of the few remaining places in the Solent where it is still possible for yachts to anchor. This is permitted in the first long reach between Lepe House and Need's Ore Pt, which provides over a mile of water sheltered by land on the north side and on the south by Beaulieu Spit, except for a swell at the eastern end at HW in strong southerly winds. Nearest landings are on the beach at the entrance, at the quay up Exbury creek, which dries at half tide, and at Need's Ore, where the club house of the Beaulieu River SC is nearby. The anchorage is far from facilities but the 2 miles up the river to Bucklers Hard do not take long with the aid of an outboard engine. A riding light is advisable as the channel is used at night. Anchorage outside the river entrance is prohibited in the cable area as indicated on the chart.

The moorings in the river are all privately rented, but there are pile moorings to accommodate about 100 visiting yachts. Application for a berth, or for the use of a mooring

5.3.   Starboard pile No 15 and the entrance to
       Exbury Creek.

5.5.    Gin's Farm. R Southampton YC in the background.

5.6.    Bucklers Hard. The marina is about a cable beyond the jetty.

if temporarily available, should be made to the Harbour Master at Bucklers Hard (Mr. W. H. J. Grindey, Tel: 0590 616200/616234). His office is at the Yacht Harbour, which is only 200 m beyond the Bucklers Hard jetty. Fuel and water can be had at the marina fuelling jetty. All facilities are provided: full yacht service, maintenance and chandlery, Bucklers Hard Boatbuilders for all boatyard requirements, and Bucklers Hard Garage and Marine for servicing, overhauls and winterizing of inboard and outboard engines. Bucklers Hard Stores is open seven days a week in season and will accept telephone orders for collection, including newspapers.

5.7.    Bucklers Hard Yacht Harbour. Fuel jetty on the left.

5.8.    Bucklers Hard visitors' mooring piles.

In the small village, which consists of two widely spaced rows of cottages running down to the river, there is the Master Builder's House Hotel with bars and a restaurant. The Maritime Museum (which is well worth seeing) is at the far end on the left, where there is the car park and The Mainsail for light lunches and snacks. A footpath provides a pleasant walk along the river and through the woods to Beaulieu.

At Beaulieu, landing can be made at high water. There is 1.5 m at Timbrell's Quay, where there is the Palace Quay boatyard. The Abbey, and Palace House and gardens and Motor Museum are open to visitors and there are a few shops, PO and an hotel.

# 6 Cowes and Medina River

**High Water** (Long): Springs mean −0 h 15 m Portsmouth; Neaps mean +0 h 15 m.
**Tidal Heights:** MHWS 4.2 m MLWS 0.6 m MHWN 3.5 m MLWN 1.7 m.
**Stream sets** to the westward in Cowes Roads 1 h 30 m before local HW and to the eastward just before LW.
**Depths:** Except for a 1.5 m patch opposite East Cowes SC, there is a minimum of 2.4 m in the channel to within ½ mile of the Folly Inn, when depths fall to 0.9 m and then to 0.3 m off the light beacon, beyond which the channel soon dries out.
**Yacht Clubs:** Royal Yacht Squadron, Royal London Yacht Club, Island Sailing Club, East Cowes Sailing Club, Cowes Corinthian Yacht Club, Castle Rock Sailing Club.

THE DAYS OF the great schooners and cutters, with their famous owners and big professional crews, are long past and with them something of the splendour of Cowes has gone. Today the scene is basically amateur but infinitely broader and more active with the vast fleets of smaller yachts. Cowes Week, when coupled with the start of the Fastnet Race, provides the highlight which attracts yachtsmen the world over and creates what is probably the greatest and most vivid spectacle in international yacht racing.

Cowes is conveniently centred near the middle of the northern Island shore and at no time in its history has the town been more dedicated to yachting and providing amenities for visiting yachtsmen.

**Approach and Entrance**

Approach from the west is easy by following the line of the coast from Egypt Point about 200 m offshore or less according to the state of the tide and draught of the yacht. As racing men know, sometimes to their cost, there are rocky edges extending in places almost 100 m seawards. The streams are strong. When approaching from the west, or leaving the harbour bound west, an early eddy running contrary to the main flood stream will be found inshore between the Squadron and Egypt Point.

From the eastward, keep well to seaward to avoid the Shrape Mud and shallow water N and NW of it. At night, a look out should be kept for unlit buoys.

The fairway lies on the west side of the harbour and is marked by buoys. On the east side there is a long breakwater which serves to scour the channel and to provide protection from winds from this quarter. Here the water is shallow but the area is occupied by large numbers of private moorings and yachtsmen should avoid sailing through them owing to the danger of being set by the stream on to moored yachts.

On big regatta days parts of the fairway may be busy with racing craft which, by courtesy, should be given right-of-way, especially as seconds count when they are working into position for the start of a race or approaching the finishing line. Red Funnel ferries and

6.1.    Looking directly down the entrance to the Medina. Yacht moorings on the left, with visitors' moorings in the foreground on the right. The Island Sailing Club pontoon is beneath the two prominent chimneys with the Red Funnel pier directly behind it.

6.2.    The view to the east of the approach. Prince Consort buoy extreme left and Old Castle Point on the right.

6.3.    The view to the west. Egypt Point is to the right. This is the stretch of water known as 'The Green', famous for the multitude of yachts tacking to cheat the tide during Cowes Week. The hazardous rocky outcrops can be seen in this photo taken near low water.

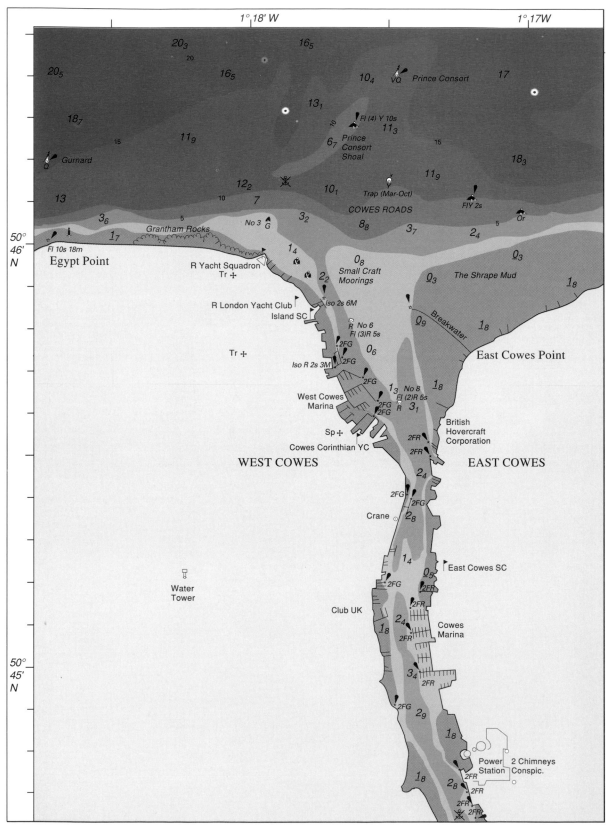

20₃   16₅   17

20   VQ Prince Consort

20₅   16₅   10₄

18₇   13₁   Fl (4) Y 10s   11₃

11₉   15   18₃

15   6₇   Prince Consort Shoal

Gurnard
Q

12₂   10₁   11₉

Trap (Mar-Oct)   Fl Y 2s

13   10   7   3₂   COWES ROADS

3₆   5   No 3 G   8₈   3₇   2₄   5   Or

Grantham Rocks   1₇

Fl 10s 18m   1₄   0₈   0₃   The Shrape Mud

**Egypt Point**   Small Craft Moorings   0₃   1₈

R Yacht Squadron Tr ✛   2₂   Breakwater

R London Yacht Club   Iso 2s 6M   0₉   1₈

Island SC   R No 6 Fl (3)R 5s   **East Cowes Point**

2FG   0₆

Tr ✛   Iso R 2s 3M   2FG

2FG   1₃   No 8   1₈   Fl (2)R 5s

West Cowes Marina   2FG   3₁ R

2FG

Sp ✛   British Hovercraft Corporation

Cowes Corinthian YC   2FR

**WEST COWES**   2FR   **EAST COWES**

2₄

2FG   2FG

Crane ◦   2₈

1₄   0₅   East Cowes SC

🖵   2FG   2FR

Water Tower   Club UK   2FR

2₄   Cowes Marina

1₈   2FR

3₄   2FR

2FG   2₉

1₈

1₈   Power Station   2 Chimneys Conspic.

2FR

1₈   2₈   2FR

2FR

**Cowes:** Soundings in metres.

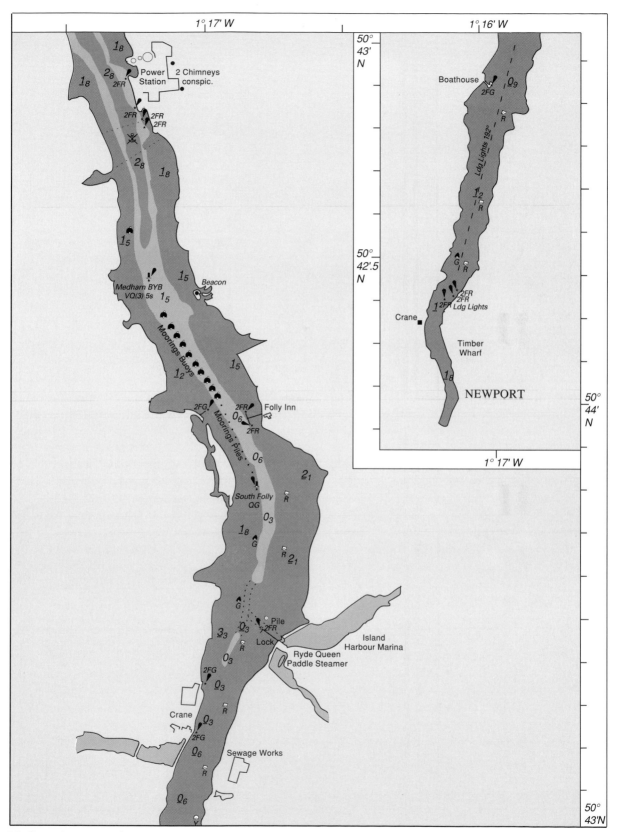

**Medina River:** Soundings in metres.

6.4.    The Royal Yacht Squadron, perhaps the most famous starting-line in the world. Behind it is
Trinity Church – often known as the yachtsman's church. It is worth visiting the memorial to
those who lost their lives in the 1979 Fastnet Race. It is situated so that you are able to view the
starting area of that ill-fated race and the stones are from the Rock itself.

high speed craft add to the congestion despite the care with which they are handled, but the
channel is easy to follow past the Island Sailing Club, the Red Funnel pontoon and the
marina. The channel narrows where the floating bridge chain ferry crosses it – and note
that the chains lie at least 0.6 m above the bottom in mid-channel. Near the floating bridge
and for a good quarter of a mile beyond it the wind is often flukey owing to high ground
and proximity of buildings. Beyond the chain ferry there are no navigation buoys but the
deep water lies in the area between the pile mooring trots and heavy moorings. Except for a
shallow patch extending across the river opposite the East Cowes SC, the minimum depth
is 2.4 m to Kingston Power Station and beyond.

The maximum speed permitted for all vessels within Cowes Harbour is 6 knots over the
ground, but speed should be reduced in the vicinity of yachts on moorings or as seamanship
requires. Water skiing and sailboarding are prohibited.

**Lights:** The Prince Consort buoy, situated about half a mile NE of the entrance, exhibits a
*V Q* light. No 3 starboard hand buoy is *FL G 3s* and No 4 port hand buoy *Q R*. The light on
the end of the breakwater is *Fl R 3s*. The leading lights in transit at 164° consist of a white
light (*Iso 2s 6M*) on the post at the seaward end of Watch House landing and a rear light
(*Iso R 2s 3M*) on the dolphin on the south side of Fountain Pier. No 6 port hand buoy is *Fl*

*(3) R.* The various wharfs and pontoons up the river exhibit vertical pairs of fixed red and green lights to port and starboard respectively. There is a *V Q (3) 5s* light on Medham beacon and a *Q G* light on the beacon south of the Folly Inn.

### Moorings and Anchorages

There are four large temporary visitors' moorings situated off the Parade, on the starboard hand just past the Royal Yacht Squadron, convenient for Customs clearance. West Cowes Marina lies on the starboard hand just beyond the Fountain Pier and the Red Funnel Pontoon. Yachts berth alongside floating pontoons close to the centre of the town and facilities, but three pile berths where yachts moor abreast of each other remain available just south of the marina. In addition, Thetis Pontoon (north of Thetis Wharf) provides alongside berthing with shore access for visiting yachts.

The swinging moorings on the east side of the harbour are private, or specially laid for racing classes during regattas, and must not be picked up by visitors. However it is sometimes possible to obtain the temporary use of one on application to the Harbour Master, Capt H N J Wrigley (Tel: 0983 293952).

As the harbour is exposed to all northerly winds it can be very uncomfortable in strong winds and gales from this quarter, when it may be better to move up the river. Visitors' moorings (clearly marked by notice boards) will be found there on both sides of the river on piles and pontoons in the reach to the south of the floating bridge to suit any size of yacht. The Cowes Marina has visitors' berths at East Cowes about a quarter of a mile above the chain ferry ('floating bridge') on the east bank of the river. There are also pile moorings for small visiting yachts in the Folly reach, opposite the Folly Inn. Beyond them is Island Harbour Marina.

Anchorage is to seaward of existing mooring buoys which lie to the east of No 4 R buoy. Cowes Roads are exposed and the streams through them are strong so the anchorage is used mostly by larger yachts. Smaller craft usually anchor in shallower water closer in to the north and NW of the end of the breakwater where there is plenty of water at neaps.

Anchors should be buoyed anywhere in the vicinity of Cowes in case of fouling mooring chains, particularly those of big commercial buoys which often stretch a long distance. The chains of the Trinity House mooring buoy, for example, extend 150 m east and west, though in the harbour the scope is much shorter. Anchorage is prohibited (1) in the fairway (2) in the mooring area on the east side of the harbour (3) where there are cables or obstructions indicated by notice boards such as just beyond the floating bridge or off Kingston Power Station (4) in the Folly Reach.

### Facilities

There are many public landings among which the following may be mentioned in order of approach: several on the Parade, Watch House Slip (nearest to Customs), two farther south

53

leading to High Street, and the south side Fountain pontoon. Whitegates pontoon is the most convenient beyond the Floating bridge. Landing is also possible by permission at various yacht yards. At East Cowes there are three slipways but at present no convenient hards or pontoons.

As stated before, Cowes is dedicated to yachting and provides exceptionally good facilities of all kinds within easy distance of the harbour. There are no less than six yacht clubs, including the Royal Yacht Squadron which remains the premier yacht club and the Island Sailing Club, which is very go-ahead and has excellent facilities with a pontoon in the season for members. It is hospitable towards foreign yachtsmen, especially to visitors in Cowes Week.

Yacht building and repairs are undertaken at Lallow's, Souter's, Cowes Marine Services and several other yards. Fuel and water are available at Lallow's jetty and the marinas, and also from a fuelling barge moored 200 m upstream of the floating bridge. There are also fresh water points at Watch House slipway, Whitegates pontoon and Old Town Quay. Among the well-known names in the yachting industry are Ratsey & Lapthorn Sailmakers, Beken's (photographs), Pascall Atkeys (chandlers) and Benzie (yachting jewellery). In addition, there are engineers and riggers and pretty well any yachting requirement is available. EC Wednesday. Customs at Watch House slip. The best-known hotel is the Fountain, but there are several others and numerous pubs and boarding houses. Cowes is a convenient harbour in which to leave a yacht under surveillance during an owner's absence by arrangement with the Harbour Master.

There is a good bus service connecting with all parts of the Island. Red Funnel steamers and high speed service to Southampton.

## River Medina

The river cuts a long groove through to the centre of the Island from Cowes to Newport, the capital. It is in part commercial, but the land in the background on either side is high and to the east it is well wooded so the scene is by no means unattractive. The channel is not buoyed but it lies between mooring piles or mooring buoys and is not difficult to follow with depths of 2.4 m to Kingston Power Station and a quarter of a mile beyond, when it becomes shallower and soon falls to 0.9 m as the Folly reach is entered. The river is spanned by submarine power cables and a pipe line, the positions being marked by notice boards to indicate prohibited anchorage.

From Kingston to the Folly Inn the channel is best followed by leaving the line of moorings and Medham Beacon close to starboard. On an ordinary spring tide yachts of 1.5 m draught can sail up to the Folly Point and there is plenty of water at neaps, though larger yachts should bring up to the piles in 1.8 m to 2.4 m about half a mile to the northward.

Off the Folly Inn there are pile moorings suitable at ordinary springs for yachts drawing 1.4 m or up to 1.8 m to 2.4 m at neaps, but anchorage is not permitted. There is a landing

6.5. The Folly Inn and public landing with dinghy pontoons on the east bank of the Medina River.

pontoon at the jetty and a scrubbing hard which can be used by arrangement at the inn, where there is a buffet bar and meals can be had to order. A water taxi runs during the summer. Fresh water is laid to the pontoon and there is a small shop. Calor gas is available. In all, it is a quiet and pleasant place to bring up.

The Island Harbour Marina lies about half a mile south of the Folly Inn with berths for 240 yachts in the locked basin. The approach channel marked by port hand piles and starboard buoys is dredged to 0.9 m MLWS. The depth in the basin is maintained at about 2.4 m. The lock is operated on request 3 hours either side of high water when 2.4 m of water will be found. It is not normally lit but can be floodlit if a yacht is expected at night (Tel: 0983 526020). Facilities at the marina are not extensive, but it more than makes up for this by its largely unspoilt rural setting. There is an attractive riverside footpath to Newport.

Above the Folly the depths soon begin to decrease but the river is navigable with sufficient rise of tide by ships to Newport. The upper reaches provide interesting sailing. There are pontoons for bilge-keel craft at Newport (EC Thursday).

6.6. The visitors' pontoon at Newport.

# 7 Southampton Water

**Double High Water:** Springs −0 h 30 m and +1 h 30 m Portsmouth; Neaps mean +0 h 15 m. At Springs after about 3 hours flood there is a stand for 1.5 hours, followed by a 3.5 hours rise. The ebb runs strongly for 3.5 hours attaining maximum rate 2 hours after second HW.
**Tidal Heights:** Southampton, above datum. MHWS 4 m MLWS 0.5 m MHWN 3.7 m MLWN 1.8 m.
**Depths:** Ample at any state of the tide.
**Yacht Clubs:** R Southampton YC, Southampton SC, Ashlett SC, Eling SC, Hythe SC, Marchwood YC, Netley Cliff SC, Weston SC, Weston CC, Netley SC(ASA), Esso (Fawley) SC, Fawley Power Station SC, Cracknore Hard SC.

WITH ITS DEEP and easy approach and double high water, Southampton has been a natural port and centre of shipbuilding from time immemorial. Inevitably too, it has been an objective of raids from the sea by Danes and the French. Nevertheless, it was the Norman Conquest which brought greatly increased trade to Southampton. The Bargate was built and the prosperous part of the town lay between this and the present Royal Pier, where some of it is still to be seen. The Middle Ages brought increased prosperity, especially in the wool and wine trades. It was not until the middle of the eighteenth century that the port began its modern development and from then onwards grew rapidly in stature.

In particular, the name of Southampton has been linked with those of the great transatlantic liners. It was the home port of many famous ships, among which were the ill-fated *Titanic*, the *Mauretania* and *Lusitania* and the Queens, *Mary*, *Elizabeth* and *Elizabeth II*, besides their competitors among the great ships of the world seeking the honour of the Blue Riband. Southampton remains a port for many of the leading cruise lines but the majority of shipping is now container and cargo carrying. The importance of the port is increased by the huge oil refinery at Fawley and the petroleum terminal on the opposite side of Southampton Water.

Southampton Water provides a considerable length for day cruising with the added interest of its shipping. The port itself and the city are the administrative centre of the whole area, with Customs, Lloyds Surveyors and the Department of Transport for the registration of yachts as well as of ships. The town offers every kind of yachting facility.

## Main Approaches

That part of the Solent which lies to the south of Southampton Water is wide and exposed, especially in southwesterly gales. The area between Hill Head and Calshot should be treated with respect in any strength of wind from the north west since considerable gusts are often experienced.

The most frequent cause of problems for yachtsmen is the Bramble Bank, which although clearly marked by many buoys and the orange Bramble Beacon, often seems to lure the unwary navigator on to its unforgiving sand. The part of it that dries and is

7.1. The West Bramble buoy around which many large ships turn when making for Fawley or Southampton. Viewed from the east, the distant buoy is NE Gurnard.

therefore the most hazardous lies approximately 500 m to the north west of the Bramble Beacon and 100 m east of the small green conical 'West Knoll' buoy. Its extent can be gauged by the fact that an annual cricket match takes place upon it between a team from Cowes and another from the mainland.

The area to the east of the bank is generally shallow and an eye should be kept on the echo sounder whilst sailing in this vicinity. If the tide is such that you have cause to be concerned about depth, stay north of a line between West Bramble (*West Cardinal V Q (9) 10s*), West Knoll (*G Conical*), East Knoll (*C Conical*) and Hill Head (*R Can Fl R 5s*) or to the south of a line between West Bramble, Bramble Beacon (orange pile) and East Bramble (*East Cardinal VQ (3) 5s*).

In many respects the Bramble Bank can be imagined as the hub of an often busy two-way roundabout. Most of the shipping using either Southampton or Fawley enters the Solent from the east and follows the deep water channel in a westerly direction until turning around the Bramble on to a north easterly heading and into the Thorn Channel. To enter Southampton Water, a further tight turn to the north west is made around Calshot. This is certainly not the place to get anywhere near shipping since their course allows no room for manoeuvre.

7.2. The Bramble Bank viewed from just north of west. The shallowest part lies between West Knoll buoy in the foreground and the Bramble beacon almost directly behind it.

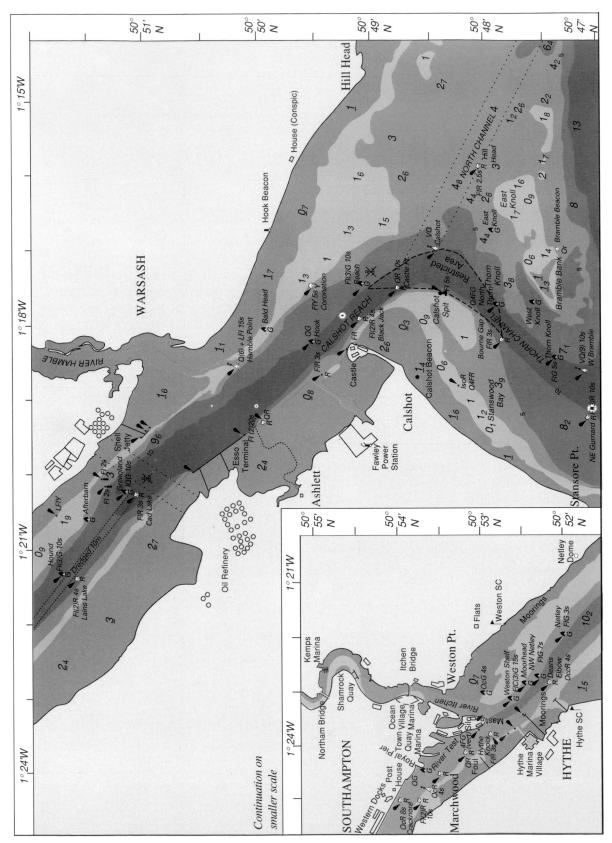

**Southampton Water:** Soundings in metres.

*Continuation on smaller scale*

## Main chart (upper)

WARSASH

RIVER HAMBLE

Hamble Point

Hill Head

House (Conspic)

Hook Beacon

Bald Head

Coronation

CALSHOT REACH

Castle Pt.

Castle

Black Jack

Calshot Spit

Calshot

Calshot Beacon

Calshot Station

Stanswood Bay

Fawley Power Station

Ashlett

Esso Terminal

Shell Jetty

Greenland

Afterbarn

Cad Lake

Lains Lake

Hound

Oil Refinery

Restricted Area

NORTH CHANNEL 4

THORN CHANNEL

Bourne Gap

Thorn Knoll

West Knoll

Thorn Knoll

East Knoll

East Knoll

Bramble Bank

Bramble Beacon

Stansore Pt.

NE Gurnard R

W Bramble

## Inset chart (lower)

SOUTHAMPTON

Western Docks

Northam Bridge

Kemps Marina

Shamrock Quay

Ocean Village

Town Quay Marina

Royal Pier

Post House

River Itchen

River Test

Itchen Bridge

Weston Pt.

Weston SC

Flats

Weston Shelf

Marchwood

Hythe Pier

Hythe Marina Village

HYTHE

Hythe SC

Moorings

Moorhead

NW Netley

Netley

Netley Dome

Deans Elbow

Crackmore

Foul

Hythe Knock

Mastmoorings

7.3.   The Calshot Spit light-float seen from the south east. The massive structure of Fawley power station dominates this area; it is, however, a useful wind indication and when its acrid emissions lie horizontal, better think of a reef.

## Main Approaches

The Southampton Dock Board southern boundary line runs from Stansore Point to Hill Head and there is a port bye-law which reads: 'It has been found necessary to restrict small craft from that part of the main navigable channel . . . which lies between a line drawn from Bourne cap to North Thorn Buoy and a line drawn from Castle Point Buoy to Reach Buoy' (see chart). 'The transit and movement of small craft under 20 m LOA through the above area when vessels of over 100 m LOA are navigating the Western Approach Channel (including the Thorn Channel and Calshot Reach) between West Bramble Buoy and Hook Buoy WILL NOT BE PERMITTED.

To assist those small craft, Southampton Vessel Traffic Services Centre (call sign SOUTHAMPTON VTS) will make a Traffic Information Broadcast on VHF Channel 12 every two hours on the hour from 0600 to 2200, Fridays to Sundays inclusive and Bank Holiday Mondays, from Easter to the last weekend of major events.' Anchorage in the fairway including the Test and Itchen is also forbidden. The bye-laws should be strictly observed as, apart from the law, it is only common sense to keep out of the way of vessels, particularly tankers, which are very difficult to manoeuvre in the narrow water available for their deep draught, and which are virtually impossible to stop quickly.

So far as yacht racing is concerned, the problem has to some extent been relieved by the laying of special buoys, which provide turning-marks clear of the deep channels. The problem should be a lesser one when cruising, as there is plenty of room in the approaches to Southampton to navigate either outside the deep fairways or on the edge of them without obstructing the big ships, crossing the fairways only when the channel is clear. What is important is to anticipate the movements of the big ships. Leaving Southampton Water and rounding usually close east of Calshot Light Float, they proceed down the Western Approach Channel. Thence they continue either in deep water west to the Needles (Signal W over Answering pennant) or they round the West Bramble buoy, turning to pass between the South Bramble and Prince Consort Buoy and east to Spithead. (Signal E over Answering pennant.) Smaller ships may proceed east via the North Channel. Should a ship be hampered by a smaller vessel she will sound five or more short blasts (ColReg 34d). In poor visibility she would – like a yacht under sail – be sounding one long followed by two short blasts at intervals of no more than two minutes (ColReg 35c), whether or not other vessels are known to be in the vicinity.

Approaching from the west a good offing should be given to the shoals off Stone and Stansore Points, leaving to port three beacons, Q R, situated near the 5 m line. Do not steer direct from the westerly beacon to the next at LW as the shoal bulges about 50 yards seaward between them. Power cables (from 33,000 to 132,000 volts), telephone cables and gas pipes cross the Solent from shore to shore on this prohibited anchorage, which extends approximately from Lepe to Gurnard Head on the west side and between Stansore Point and Egypt Point on the east. Damage can be caused even by a small yacht attempting to winch up an anchor fouled on a cable or by impact or grounding on a cable in shallow water such as lies northward of the three beacons. The owner of a yacht causing damage to a cable may render himself liable for loss and repair costs running into a very large sum.

The Western Approach for big ships lies between the flats off the Hampshire coast and the Bramble Bank. On the NW side it is marked by NE Gurnard buoy (*Fl (3) R 10s*) and Bourne Gap buoy (*Fl R 3s*) and Calshot Spit light-float (*Fl 5s Horn (2)*). There is plenty of water for most yachts west of the buoys as shown on the chart, but Calshot Spit dries out in a SE direction for half a mile from the beach and most Solent yachts leave the light-float

7.4.    Calshot Spit light-float with the radar tower and Calshot Castle behind it. It is part of the area in which the movement of small vessels is restricted (see text).

about 200 m and Castle Point buoy (*I Q R 10s*) 100 m to starboard, which gives 2 m at MLWS. Greater liberties can be taken with sufficient rise of tide. The next red port hand buoy is Black Jack (*Fl (2) R 4s*) but this is near the NE edge of Calshot Spit so it should either be passed on the correct side or left very close to starboard. Beyond this buoy the water deepens and course may be laid to leave Calshot Castle jetty to port or to cross over to the east side of Southampton Water either to proceed to Hamble or up to Southampton.

On the SE side the Western Approach is marked by the West Bramble (*V Q (9) 10s*), Thorn Knoll (*Fl G 5s*), North Thorn (*Q G*) and Calshot (*V Q*) buoys. On this side also, yachts can avoid the fairway by going on the wrong side of these buoys, and leaving the yellow Spanker and green W Knoll and E Knoll buoys to starboard.

At night it is simplest to keep in or near to Western Approach channel as it is clearly marked by the light buoys shown on the chart. During fog, pilotage is assisted by the bell, *15s*, on W Bramble, the Horn (2) on Calshot light-float and the bell, *30s* on Calshot N Car Buoy.

From the east the approach is equally easy. The channel lies between the land with its offlying shoals on the starboard hand and the buoys on the east side of the Brambles: E Bramble (*V Q (3) 5s*), Hill Head (*Fl R 2.5s*). Yachts can pass up to a quarter of a mile eastward of the Calshot buoy (*V Q*) and *Bell 30s*, in 4.6 m. The Coronation Y conical buoy (*Fl Y 5s*) is starboard hand but may be left close to port at most states of the tide. The small G conical Bald Head starboard hand buoy is moored close to the drying shoal extending off the shore.

### The Main Channel

Southampton Water main shipping channel is marked on the port hand (west side) by red can buoys exhibiting *Oc R* or *Fl R* lights, there are also lights at either end of Fawley jetty (2 *FR vert*). The starboard (east side) is marked by conical green buoys showing *Fl G* lights. In addition, there are occasional R (port) and G (starboard) buoys nearer the edge of the mud

7.5.   Calshot Spit Radar Tower and pier on the left. The view to the south west on entering Southampton Water.

7.6.   Looking up Southampton Water. The Esso Marine Terminal on the left and the Shell Mex
       Jetty and entrance to the Hamble River to the right.

for the use of ships of less draught. The channel itself is clear and wide and the general
direction up to the Dockhead is north-westerly.

On the west side of Southampton Water, after passing Calshot Castle, the Esso Refinery
jetties are the first conspicuous features, and extend a long way from the shore, on which
large oil reservoirs will be seen. At night the whole area is illuminated by the lights and the
glare of the excess gas flare stacks reflected in the clouds. For the next two miles beyond the
refineries the west shore possesses no particular features except for the measured distance
beacons with white triangles situated high on the mud flats. Three red buoys are passed and
westward of the third is the Admiralty jetty (2 *FR*), for the old Coastal Forces Base off
which there are many large mooring buoys. The Hythe Sailing Club is on the shore just
south of it. Hythe ferry pier lies about half a mile beyond the Admiralty jetty and once past
this the deep channel lies on the east side near the docks.

The starboard hand (east) of Southampton Water is equally clearly marked. Once inside
Calshot, after passing the Reach buoy (*Fl (3) G 10s*), the first buoy on the starboard hand is
the Hook (*Q G and bell*) but this lies on the edge of the big ship fairway, and from a
yachtsman's point of view may almost be considered as placed in mid-channel. Half a mile
east of the Hook is the Coronation buoy, previously mentioned. Hamble Point S Car buoy
(*Q (6) + L Fl 15s*) is nearly a mile farther up, marking the port side of the entrance to
Hamble River, but it is a starboard buoy when proceeding up Southampton Water. On
Hamble Point will be seen the Cougar Marine works, and about a mile farther up will be
seen a number of oil storage tanks and the Shell Jetty. Hamble Spit, which dries out at CD,
projects into Southampton Water approximately to a line from Hamble Point Buoy to the
end of the Shell Jetty and should be left well to starboard. In summer months it is marked
by the yellow Cathead racing buoy.

Following up the line of the coast for another two miles, the site of the Royal Victoria
Hospital at Netley, of which only the central dome remains, is brought abeam. Above

7.7.  The Fawley oil terminals on the west side of Southampton Water, opposite to the Hamble River.

Netley the mud runs out a greater distance from the shore and Weston Shelf dries out at CD. At low water even a yacht of light draught will have to keep near to the buoyed channel.

At the Dockhead, which is conspicuous in the middle of Southampton Water, the channel divides, the River Test continuing in a NW direction and the River Itchen branching away to the NNE. These rivers are referred to under separate headings.

**Fawley Basin.** The entrance to the dredged channel leading to the Fawley Power Station lies about a quarter of a mile beyond Calshot Castle on the west side of Southampton Water. It is very clearly marked by pile beacons, with occasional lights at night when in use by ships. There are moorings for local yachts, belonging to members of the Fawley Power Station Social and Sports Club, on the south side between No 10 beacon and the entrance channel and water intake of the Power Station. Across this entrance there is a floating oil boom, the apex of which is secured by anchors with buoys, which are sometimes mistaken by strangers for mooring buoys. Yachts must keep clear of the boom, as there is an undercurrent into the channel. It may be possible on application to obtain the use of a vacant mooring or to anchor close to the port hand beacons temporarily but the slope of the mud is very steep. Visiting yachts must on no account obstruct ships using the dredged channel to the power station, and enquiry should be made about their movements.

**Ashlett Creek.** The entrance to this creek lies a mile north-west of Calshot Castle and is close to the Fawley R buoy (Q R) which lies 200 m south-west of the southern end of the Esso jetties. The creek appears to be 100 m wide at high water but most of it is very shallow, drying up to 2.4 m near Ashlett, except for a very narrow channel which is little more than a gutter winding through the mud. Nevertheless, it provides interesting water for centre-board and shallow draught craft. The active Esso (Fawley) Sailing Club has a club house near the head of the creek; it is the authority that maintains the navigation and (seasonal) racing marks in the creek.

Keel yachts can use the channel with sufficient rise of tide, but 1.2 m draught is about the maximum without local knowledge, as the channel is difficult to follow at HW springs when the marshes are covered. At low water, keel yachts must sit in mud or dry out alongside the quay.

When entering, leave Fawley buoy (which is in shallow water) close to port and come on to a course of approx 254°. Unfortunately the leading marks that used to give this transit no longer exist. Ahead will be seen the first of three small R can buoys. Follow the three R port hand buoys Nos 2, 4 and 6 round the first 90° bend into the SE reach, then round the G starboard hand buoy No 7 at the second 90° bend into a long reach to the SW. The channel is very narrow at this bend and one should keep close to the buoy. The next leg is nearly straight. In addition to the four numbered buoys, R and G posts with square and triangular topmarks mark the channel, but these are placed well up on the mud.

The third 90° bend is to NW, the channel being close to the stern moorings of the boats at the SW bank. Keep well clear of the speed limit Notice Board on the starboard hand as there is a short gravel spit running SW of it. Pass close to the post with R square top-mark, which is just north of the end of the public landing stage steps and the Esso (Fawley) Sailing Club jetty and pontoons. The channel curves slightly in a thin 'S' bend to a sharp hairpin bend round a post with R square top-mark which leave close to port. After rounding this, head straight back towards the club flagstaff and jetty, then follow the line of moorings to starboard, leaving the SLIP buoy (R) to port. Visiting yachts should now head for the public quay at the head of the creek, with moorings to starboard and mud berths to port.

There is also a South Channel, along the line of the Outfall marked by Y beacons, south of the main creek, but this should not be attempted without local knowledge.

Ashlett is pretty and consists of a quay and hard, a few houses, the old mill and The Jolly Sailor Inn. Yachts can berth at the quay which dries 2.1 m CD, and which is suitable for a scrub. Launching site at hard. Water at the Inn, stores at Fawley, half a mile distant.


### Hythe Marina Village

This development is built on reclaimed land just north west of Hythe. The entrance is marked by piles, the outer pair comprising an east cardinal mark (Q (3) 10s) and a port hand mark (Fl R (2) 5s). The channel, dredged to 2 m, leads to lock gates which are generally opened on demand. Visitors are welcome and all the usual facilities are available. See also Appendix 2: Marinas and their Facilities


### Moorings and Anchorages

Anchorage is possible in Southampton Water anywhere clear of the ship fairways and moorings and outside the prohibited areas. Anchorage should be sought under a weather shore, according to the wind, and it is wise to buoy the anchor to avoid foul mooring chains or foul bottom. Swell is caused by passing ships. The following are the places most commonly used:

1. *Hamble River.* See Chapter 8.

7.8.  Netley Great Dome with the Netley Cliff SC below.

7.9.  Ashlett Mill (now an Esso club) and the quay at high water.

7.10.  The Esso SC at Ashlett.

2. *Netley*. Half a mile north of Netley Dome, there is a good hard. Stores at Netley and bus service. Moorings for small local yachts. The anchorage lies outside these on a lee shore in westerly winds.

3. *Hythe*. Between the line of Hythe Pier and the Admiralty Jetty there is only from 0.3 to 0.9 m CD. Farther out from the shore there is 1.5 to 1.8 m. The anchorage is reasonable in westerly winds but take care to anchor clear of moorings. Landing is at Hythe pierhead, from which ferries run to Southampton and an electric train to the shore. The Hythe Sailing Club is at the shore end of the Admiralty Jetty, to the south of which the Club has many small moorings. In Hythe itself there is an hotel, shops and facilities of a small town. EC Wednesday.

4. *Rivers Test and Itchen*. See following section.

## Facilities

The recent rapid development of marina complexes on the old commercial waterfronts means that there is every facility available to yachtsmen. The shopping area near the Bar Gate is one of the best in the South of England and much of the old town has been restored to the style of its medieval beginnings.

The train service is excellent, London being just over an hour and other major cities such as Salisbury, Bristol and Portsmouth within short journey times. Alternatively, express bus services can be taken from the coach station, next to the swimming pool near the Royal Pier.

Cowes is only 20 minutes by high speed vessel or an hour by car-ferry – both run from the Royal Pier.

The Southampton Weather Centre (Tel: 0703 228844) will give the latest forecast and information.

*The Yachtsman's Guide to Southampton Water and its Approaches*, published annually by Associated British Ports is freely available and full of useful information.

## Rivers Test and Itchen

There is a 6 knot speed limit within both these rivers.

**The River Test.** Leaving the Dockhead to starboard and proceeding up the River Test in a NW direction, the Queen Elizabeth II Terminal and the Ocean Dock will be seen to starboard. The deep channel lies on the docks side of the river, whereas beyond the port hand red buoys there is the Gymp shoal and foul ground.

Continuing up the river the Town Quay Marina (due for completion 1992/3) and Royal Pier will be passed and half-a-mile farther up the river divides into two parts, leaving a narrow shoal between the two. The northern is the deep dredged channel running past the Western Docks, at the end of which is the King George V graving dock and Prince Charles Container Port. The southern side is the Marchwood Channel, and leads up past Cracknore

7.11    The southerly point of Southampton Docks. River Test to port. River Itchen to starboard.

7.12.    The southernmost of the leading beacons for the Marchwood Channel.

7.13.    The more northerly leading beacon for the Marchwood Channel. It is often obscured by moored yachts.

Hard, Husband's jetty and SW to Marchwood Basin.

To follow the southern part of the river, alter course off the Royal Pier to leave No 2 Swinging Ground red can buoy (*Fl (2) R 10s*) to port. The yacht will then come on to the leading marks for the dredged Marchwood Channel. These are two beacons, the front with a triangle topmark and the rear with a diamond topmark. Keeping these in transit at 298°, a Y can buoy (marking the NE corner of the basin dredged to Marchwood Power Station quay) will be left to port and a beacon with a square topmark to starboard. The latter stands in the middle of the shoal between the Marchwood Channel and the northern channel along the docks.

The dredged area of the Marchwood Channel, which leads only to the entrance of Marchwood Basin, ends about 200 m east of the beacon with triangle top. Here, treat the two beacons as starboard hand marks, passing close to them sailing through the area of the

Marchwood YC moorings where the shallowest lie in 0.3 m CD. Well to starboard will be seen No 4 and No 6 red Swinging Ground buoys, which are on the north side of the middle ground.

After passing the second beacon bear to port, leaving No 8 Swinging Ground buoy to port, to enter the dredged channel for the new container berths.

Alternatively, instead of following the Marchwood Channel, the northern deep ship channel can be used, finally shaping a course leaving No 8 Swinging Ground buoy to port and entering the dredged channel and swinging ground.

Then follow up the river channel, marked by beacons, until arriving at a S Car YB beacon which marks the junction of two channels.

The northern arm, which is the Test River, leads to Redbridge Wharf. It is marked by appropriate beacons, but it dries out and is of little interest except for centreboard sailing. The western arm leads to Eling where shoal draught yachts can dry out on the mud. Leave the junction beacon and also the five beacons with triangle topmarks to starboard. The channel is extremely narrow and dries 0.6 m at CD close to banks which dry 2.1 m. Just short of Eling, after passing under power cables, it turns sharply to the SW into the basin where the best water is on the starboard side. In the middle of the basin is a mud bank, between the shallow gutters of water on the north and south sides. Strangers may find the north side easier, passing the big quay and bringing up at or before the small quay, alongside which there is about 1.8 m at HW springs. Local advice is needed if wishing to remain at low water as the basin is crowded by light draught yachts and small craft. Shops in the built-up area on the north side. EC Wednesday. Launching site at hard on north side. Eling SC has a landing pontoon, winter quarters and scrubbing hard for the use of members. The Anchor Inn overlooks the basin.

The R Corps of Transport Depot and the R Engineer YC have moorings for their members' yachts downstream of Husband's Shipyard and Marchwood YC has the mooring in the area south of the transit beacons for the Marchwood Channel. The latter has its club house and a slip at the hard beyond Marchwood Power Station. Enquiries about the possibility of temporary vacant moorings may be made at Husband's shipyard or the club. The shipyard is principally commercial, but also undertakes yacht repairs, especially of large yachts. The yard supplies fuel and water and has a ferry launch to Southampton Town Quay. There is a likelihood of commercial development both on and offshore in the vicinity of Husbands Shipyard over the next few years.

**The River Itchen.** This river now accommodates three marinas and has become much used by yachts.

The entrance lies on the east side of the Dockhead between the docks and the mud flats on the starboard hand marked by Weston Shelf conical green buoy (*Fl (3) G 15s*), No 1 Swinging Ground green buoy (*Oc G 4s*) and two dolphins No 1 (*Q G*) and No 2 (*Fl G 5s*) and the Weston jetty (*2 F G vert*), beyond which is No 3 dolphin (*Fl G 7s*) and No 4 (*Q G*), while to port there is the Bank beacon (*Q R*) and the entrance to Ocean Village Marina. This occupies what was formerly the Princess Alexandra Dock, and traffic through the narrow entrance is controlled by light signals: *2FG over 1FW* = TWO WAY TRAFFIC; *3 FR* = ALL STOP.

About a mile from the entrance, the Itchen bridge (24.4 m) crosses the river. The river then bears NW and is marked on the port hand by Crosshouse beacon (*Oc R 5s*) and a little farther up by Chapel beacon (*Fl G 3s*) on the starboard hand, opposite the Victoria Wharf jetty (*2 F R vert*).

The channel starts a bend to the north east, the deep water being on the west side. About half a mile upstream the Shamrock Quay Marina is located on the port hand in the old Camper & Nicholson premises. There is then a semi-circular bend right round to the west which is marked by beacons. Various pontoons are left to starboard before arriving off Kemps Quay Marina, also left to starboard. Beyond this the river leads east for about a quarter of a mile to Northam Bridge with the channel on the south side and a very wide expanse of mud on the north. Beyond the road bridge the Itchen is only 0.6 to 0.9 m deep and not marked.

Details of all three marinas will be found in Appendix 2: Marinas and their Facilities.

7.14.   Shamrock Quay Marina.

# 8 Hamble River and Titchfield Haven

**Double High Water:** Springs −0 h 25 m and +1 h 35 m Portsmouth; Neaps mean +0 h 20 m. At springs after about 3 hours flood there is a stand for 1.5 hours, followed by a 3.5 hours rise. The ebb runs strongly for 3.5 hours attaining maximum rate 2 hours after second HW.

**Tidal Heights above datum** at Calshot Castle: MHWS 4.4 m MLWS 0.6 m MHWN 3.6 m MLWN 1.8 m.

**Stream sets** in the Solent west about −1 h 0 m Portsmouth and east shortly after +4 h 0 m. Note an early stream sets SE at about +3 h 0 m. Portsmouth on the east side of the entrance to Southampton Water opposite Calshot LV when the main Solent stream is still running west.

**Depths above datum:** For the average yacht of 1.8 m draught, the Hamble River is deep, but in reality the bottom is very uneven, much of it being 3.6 m and more, with shoal patches such as in the vicinity of the Spit Pile 1.5 m at CD and only 2.4 m off the School of Navigation pier. For this reason it is best to take the depth as 2.1 m which gives about 2.7 m at MLWS up to Badman Creek. Above this there is something in the nature of a bar with only 1.5 m, after which the depths are 1.8 to 2.1 m up to Bursledon Bridge.

**Yacht Clubs:** R Southern YC, R Thames YC, R Air Force YC, Household Division YC, Hamble River SC, Warsash SC.

FOR A CONSIDERABLE time the Hamble River has been one of the largest concentrated yachting centres in the British Isles, and the river is packed with yachts the whole two and a half miles from Hamble Point Quay near the entrance up to Bursledon Bridge. In addition to rows of pile moorings, there are five large and well equipped marinas. What is so interesting is the extraordinary variety of yachts in the river. There are many famous ocean racers and new yachts of every kind to the latest designs, both sail and power, besides great numbers of first rate cruising yachts. Smaller standard types can be counted by the hundred

8.1.   The entrance is well marked with piles.

and the picture is broadened by old-timers and other yachts of individual character.

Historically, the river, in common with other Solent harbours, has been the scene of many attacks by invaders from the sea. Cedric and Cynric are said to have landed in the year 519 – the year in which the final defeat of the Britons took place. It is certain that it was much attacked in later years by the Danes. Swanwick is one of the place names in Hampshire which are probably of Danish origin – perhaps originally Sweinwyk.

Motor yachts and yachts under auxiliary power must keep to starboard side of the fairway and navigate with care and at a speed such as will not cause damage or danger. Speeds should certainly be low, otherwise the wash causes the utmost inconvenience to those aboard the hundreds of yachts on moorings and can be a danger to children in boats.

**The Approach and Channel**

The sailing directions for Southampton Water will bring a yacht inside Calshot Castle, when course should be shaped for the Hook green pillar buoy (*Q G*), which lies in the centre of Southampton Water about a quarter of a mile NE of Calshot Castle. From this point, Hamble Point Buoy is situated NW only only three quarters of a mile distant. When approaching from the east, the Hook will be left to the westward, and course set to leave the Coronation Buoy (*Fl Y 5s*) to starboard, or very close to port, as it is not far off the shoal on the east side of Southampton Water. The unlit Baldhead Buoy (G) must be left to starboard.

When Hamble Point S Car Buoy (*Q (6) + L Fl 15s*) is brought abeam, a series of piles marking the channel will be seen. These make the channel clear, but if a transit is desired it will be a red diamond day mark on Pile No 6 beacon on the port side of the channel in line 345° with a red triangle day mark on a white pole beacon. The port hand piles are fluorescent red with can tops and are marked with even numbers 2, 4, 6, 8 and 10. Do not bring these port hand marks too close aboard. The starboard hand piles are green with green triangular topmarks. They bear odd numbers from 1 to 9, and also should not be approached closely.

The channel bends towards the NE at No 6 pile and the inner entrance to the river is between Hamble Point Quay on the port hand and the end of the Warsash Jetty on the starboard hand. Here the fairway is on the starboard side of the river. Once inside the river

8.2  The inner entrance of the river with Hamble Point Quay on the port side. The Harbour Master's office at Warsash can just be seen on the right of the picture.

8.3.    The rather startling end of the Warsash Jetty.

there are fewer navigation marks, but the channel is fairly obvious as there are numbers of yachts moored on both sides of the fairway.

The village of Warsash lies to starboard, where will be seen the prominent black and white Harbour Master's office building and his pier. Opposite Warsash there is the Hamble Point Marina. A ferry service, dating from some 500 years, still operates between Warsash and Hamble. Hamble itself is about half a mile farther up the river on the port hand. The Royal Southern YC, RAFYC and Port Hamble Marina will be seen to port.

The bends in the river are shown on the chart. As the first bend to the NNW is approached about a quarter of a mile above the Port Hamble Marina there was an isolated gravel bank. Many yachts used to run aground on this but it is now west of the port hand piles. Also on the port hand, just before Badnam Creek, yachtsmen will find the Mercury Yacht Harbour, and beyond it the extensive Lincegrove Marsh, which is broken up into many small shallow creeks. On the opposite side of the river is a beacon (*FL G 2s*) and tide gauge marking the edge of the extensive mud flats on the starboard hand. The river then takes a NE direction to Swanwick and the fairway lies between mooring piles on either hand.

At the end of this reach is a sharp turn from NE to NW and a stranger approaching the bend will see yachts apparently lying to piles in the middle of the river and more yachts not far from them lying on moorings on the east side. This is because there is a mud shoal at the bend on the port side extending almost halfway across the river, marked by a red beacon (*Fl R 2s*). This must be left to port as also the line of mooring piles beyond it, but the yachts on moorings are left to starboard.

8.4.    Warsash and the Harbour Master's modern office building and his pier in the foreground.

8.5. The fuelling berth at Hamble Point Marina.

8.6. The sharp bend at Swanwick shore leading to Moody's yard and Swanwick Marina.

Above Bursledon Point there are two short reaches; first, NW to Bursledon leaving Moody's Swanwick Marina to starboard and then NE up to the bridge. The deep channel is much narrower in these upper reaches and lies close to the piles on the port hand. The wind is fickle when it is blowing off the high ground on the west side. There is a shoal on the starboard side of the channel close above Swanwick Marina.

Beyond Bursledon Bridge there is a railway bridge and a motorway bridge. In the reach between them there are vessels lying on moorings. At high water the channel is navigable in a dinghy or by light draught craft as far as Botley, about three miles above the bridge; in fact, the channel is fairly wide and over a fathom deep for much of the distance. The river runs between densely wooded shores and is very pretty.

**Lights:** Leading lights are established which lead up the outer two reaches of the river channel as far as Warsash. The first pair consist of the light (*Oc (2) R 12s*) on No 6 Pile beacon in line at 345° with a rear beacon (*Q R*) on Hamble Common, which has an arc of 8°. The lights for the next transit up to Warsash are a light (*Q G*) on the Warsash Shore Beacon and a light (*Iso G 6s*) over an arc of 8° on the rear beacon, the transit being 026°. This will lead to a position abreast the Warsash Jetty (*2 FG vert*). Beyond this, the river is

73

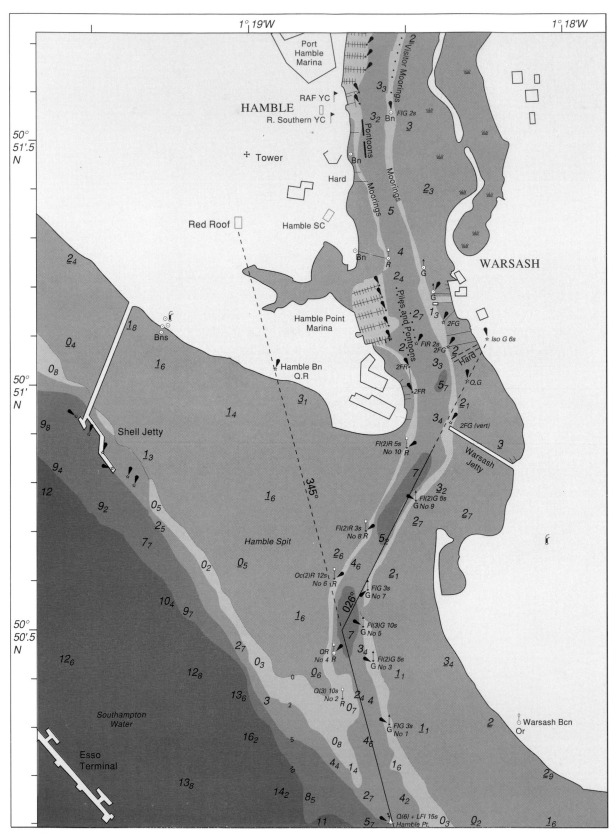

**Hamble River:** Soundings in metres.

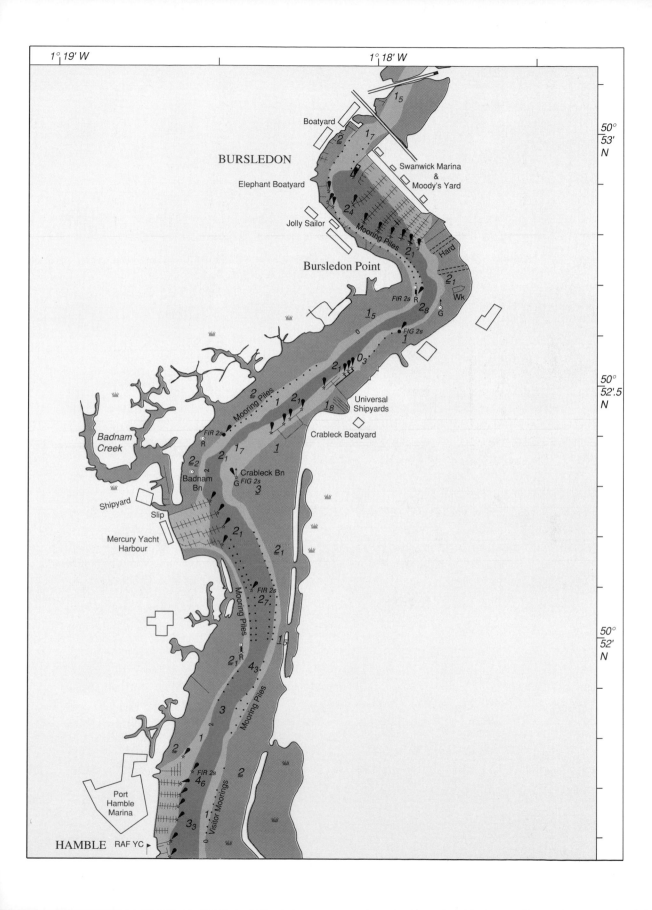

50° 53' N

Boatyard

BURSLEDON

Elephant Boatyard

Swanwick Marina & Moody's Yard

Jolly Sailor

Mooring Piles

Hard

Bursledon Point

Wk

FlR 2s  R

G

FlG 2s

50° 52'.5 N

Mooring Piles

Universal Shipyards

Badnam Creek

FlR 2s  R

Crableck Boatyard

Badnam Bn

Crableck Bn
FlG 2s

Shipyard

Slip

Mercury Yacht Harbour

FlR 2s

Mooring Piles

50° 52' N

R

Mooring Piles

FlR 2s

Port Hamble Marina

Visitor Moorings

HAMBLE  RAF YC

marked as far as Bursledon Point beacon by six lights (*Fl R 2s*) on piles on the port hand and by four lights (*Fl G 2s*) on the starboard hand, as well as many fixed lights R and G, as appropriate, marking the various jetties and pontoons.

## Moorings, Anchorage and Facilities

There is no room left in the Hamble River for anchoring, except in between No 6 port hand pile and No 9 starboard pile, clear of the leading transit. Here it is rough in fresh SW winds and during daytime it is disturbed by the wakes of constantly passing motor yachts, so it is useful only if arriving at night waiting for daylight to continue up the river.

The Harbour Master (Capt C J Nicholl OBE) and his Assistant (Mr D Walker) have an office and jetty at Warsash shore (Tel: 0489 576387). The Administrative Officer mans the office during office hours. Application should be made to the Harbour Master for berthing, but the following positions are available for visiting yachts and bear notices to this effect.

*Warsash*. Piles on the port hand of the main fairway Nos B1 to 4.

*Hamble*. Opposite Port Hamble piles on the starboard side Nos 9 to 16.

There are four public scrubbing hards. The Warsash Hard just off The Rising Sun Hotel; Hamble Hard just off the Bugle Public House; the Mercury Scrubbing Hard, where one is advised to berth N of the pile; and the Lands End Hard opposite Swanwick Marina. All four are operated on a first-come-first-served basis and free of charge for the first 48 hours.

Berths may also be available on application at Port Hamble and Swanwick marinas, as also at the Mercury Yacht Harbour and Hamble Point Marina. It is wise to book in advance. The yacht yards may also be able to advise on moorings temporarily available in the absence of their owners, and the yacht clubs have moorings which if temporarily vacant may be available, on application, to members of affiliated clubs or other approved visitors.

Water and fuel may be had at any of the yacht marinas or yacht yards. Customs' launches for clearance.

At Warsash there is a chandlery and nearby is the Rising Sun Hotel. There is a car park and hard suitable for launching. In the village there are banks, several small shops and a PO. EC Thursday. Buses to Gosport, Bursledon and Southampton.

At Hamble there is the large Port Hamble Marina with the usual marina facilities, including fuel. J. R. Williams (Chandlery) Ltd at Hamble make and repair sails. Launching sites at the public hard or Port Hamble. There are other chandlers, yacht agents, three banks and shops of most kinds in the village. EC Wednesday. Buses to Woolston, Bursledon and Southampton. The R Southern YC is close to the hard. South of this is a car park (and another is in the village) and the dinghy enclosure. The RAFYC is just south of Port Hamble Ltd at the end of the Ropewalk, and Hamble River SC by the ferry hard.

Farther up the river at Badnam Creek on the west side about three quarters of a mile from Hamble is the Mercury Yacht Harbour. There are the usual marina arrangements for water and electricity, but for repairs, laying-up, other yard work and for fuel, yachts are taken to Port Hamble. In the next reach there is the jetty (with fuel and water) of Universal

Shipyards (Solent) Ltd. At Swanwick Shore, farther up the river where it bends to NW is a public hard (launching site), the jetty and dinghy landing pontoon of A H Moody and Son Ltd.

At this old established family yard there is every conceivable facility, including yacht agency and chandlers, for yachts of all sizes. The large Swanwick Marina adjoins the yard and has been considerably extended on the NW end. Bruce Banks Sails at Sarisbury and Ian Proctor Metal Masts are in easy reach by car or bus. There is a grocer near Moody's and 100 yards up the Swanwick road is another grocer, PO and butcher. Hot and cold snacks at The Spinnaker, restaurant at the Old Ship (best to book in advance) or across the bridge at The Swan. Buses to Southampton, Fareham, Gosport and Warsash.

The village of Bursledon is a little higher up the river on the west side with landing at the steps by the Jolly Sailor or at the hard by the bridge, but the end of the latter dries out before LW. The Elephant Boat Yard is just beyond the Jolly Sailor. Launching site (often congested) at Land's End 200 m SE of the Jolly Sailor, at the bridge hard or at the boatyards above the bridges by arrangement. Grocers and PO at Old Bursledon. Restaurant at the Swan Hotel and up the hill at the Crow's Nest. Station at Bursledon, main road bus stop at the Swan and the Hamble bus stop at the Crow's Nest. Beyond the motorway bridge, on the west side, is the Upper Hamble Country Park.

8.7.    The popular Jolly Sailor opposite the Swanwick Marina.

### Titchfield Haven

Titchfield Haven lies three miles SE of the Hamble River and at the west end of Hill Head. This attractive Lilliputian harbour consists of a mud camber at the entrance of the River Meon south of the sluice under the coast road. It is protected from north and west but is very small and dries out at low water springs, so that it is only suitable for centre-board dinghies and very shoal draught yachts, such as bilge keelers which can take the bottom. Anchorage outside is possible in offshore winds but it will be far from the haven, as the sand and shingle dries out a quarter of a mile at LW springs, so that even entering it by dinghy involves a wait for sufficient rise of tide (allowing for drying 1.5 to 2.1 m at CD), except when sufficient river water is coming down.

The Camber lies behind a shingle spit, to the west of which is the coastal road above the sea wall, parking space and further west many beach chalets. To the north of the spit there is a large, white house, a clump of trees just east of it and a large red brick house with other houses farther eastwards.

8.8.   Titchfield Haven can only be approached with sufficient rise of tide over the drying sand and shingle. The modern building on the sea wall is the Hill Head SC. Opposite can be seen a small metal beacon, a race starting mark without navigational significance.

The Hill Head Sailing Club holds a prominent position on the sea wall in front of the red brick house. The best approach (which can only be made with sufficient rise of tide over the drying sand and shingle) is with the club bearing 030°. The sea wall should be approached until the entrance to the Haven opens on the port hand. Entry should be made almost parallel to the sea wall keeping to the northern side (starboard hand) of the entrance as a shingle bank builds up on the southern side. The two beacons with crossed topmarks in front of the club house are race starting marks and not navigation marks. The sailing club (Tel: 0329 664843) should be consulted if wishing to remain and dry out, as most of the camber is occupied by moorings.

A visiting yacht could lay alongside the piled wall on the south side of the camber, but this also dries out. At Hill Head, half a mile east of the haven on the bus route is the Osborne View Hotel, shops, PO, and Hill Head Chandlery.

# 9 Wootton Creek

**High Water:** Springs mean −0 h 10 m Portsmouth; Neaps +0 h 5 m.
**Tidal Heights above datum:** MHWS 4.5 m MLWS 0.7 m MHWN 3.6 m MLWN 1.7 m.
**Stream sets** outside to the westward about −1 h 30 m Portsmouth and to the eastward +4 h 20 m.
**Depths:** Dredged up to 1.8 m CD as far as the ferry terminal but silting occurs. Shallow beyond.
**Yacht Club:** Royal Victoria Yacht Club.

WOOTTON IS ONE of the Solent creeks with charm and individuality, but unfortunately of recent years there has been considerable silting in the pool which provides the only part where a visiting yacht can remain afloat at low water and it is now doubtful if even a 1.5 m draught yacht can float on neap tides.

Quarr Abbey is situated half a mile to the eastward. Very little of the old abbey itself remains beyond the ruins of the Abbot's kitchen and fragments of the wall. This was originally built in the reign of Henry I, but the present building was erected less than 100 years ago by Benedictine monks. It is said to be one of the largest buildings built of bricks, and was designed by one of the monks.

9.1.   Wootton Beacon.

9.2   (Opposite) The leading mark triangles on the west shore, if proceeding up the creek. They are not so easily seen now that there is a small wooden building behind them.

## The Approach, Entrance and Creek (see chart page 84)

The entrance to Wootton Creek lies two miles west of Ryde Pier and is clearly marked by Wootton Beacon (Q) and further beacons either side of the channel. No special directions are necessary for the approach fom the east, but, as the mud flats run out a long way, the shore must be given a wide berth. Sail from the outer end of Ryde Pier towards Barton Point, which is the point beyond King's Quay, one and a half miles east of Old Castle Point. Then, when Wootton Beacon is seen, steer in towards it.

To approach from the west, an imaginary line from Old Castle Point to the shore end of Ryde Pier will clear all dangers handsomely, and as soon as Wootton Bridge village opens up, Wootton rocks (sometimes marked by withies) will have been passed.

Having arrived off the beacons, alter course to steer up the straight channel midway between the beacons as the fairway, which is dredged to 1.8 m CD, is very narrow. There is little room for tacking and the car ferries require most of the fairway, especially at low water, when it is best to wait until the channel is clear of any ferry seen approaching. Although the channel is deep up to the ferry pier, there is no point in entering it until there is sufficient rise of tide to sail up the river or to enter the pool, which now dries at MLWS.

If continuing to the pool, then on arrival at No 7 beacon head for the end of the Ferry Pier and leave this close to port. Once past the end of the pier the yacht will be in the pool where yachts lie at the visitors' piles and visitors' moorings.

If wishing to proceed up Wootton Creek instead of to the pool, there is a turn to starboard after passing No 7 beacon. The channel is marked by a few buoys and by leading marks which can be seen on the shore below the woods to the west. These consist of two white triangles on frames (see photograph). The best indication of the channel after the leading marks is to follow the line of moored craft, leaving them to starboard. The channel is narrow but with a sufficient rise of tide a 1.1 m draught yacht can get right up to the top of the creek.

**Lights:** Wootton Beacon (Q), No 1 (Fl G 3s), No 2 (Fl (2) G 5s), No 3 (Q G).

9.3.    The Royal Victoria Yacht Club and slipway.

9.4.    The visitors' pile moorings at high water.

9.5.    The visitors' buoys at low water.

## Moorings, Anchorage and Facilities

Wootton Creek comes under the authority of the Queen's Harbour Master at Portsmouth. His authority over the allocation of moorings and navigation in the creek is exercised through a private association, the Wootton Creek Fairways Committee (Hon Sec Mr R W Perraton, The Moorings, Sloop Lane, Wootton Bridge). Advice on moorings can be obtained from the Manager of the Royal Victoria Yacht Club, Edward Goodman (Tel: 0983 882325). Yachts must not at any time anchor in the fairway or where the car ferries turn to the hard. The ferries use the channel by day and night.

Except in strong northerly or easterly winds, the pool is a good place in which to bring up. There are both mooring buoys and mooring piles for visitors. Although the pool dries at MLWS the mud is soft and yachts of moderate draught or with bilge keels can take the ground and remain upright. The Royal Victoria Yacht Club welcomes visiting yachtsmen.

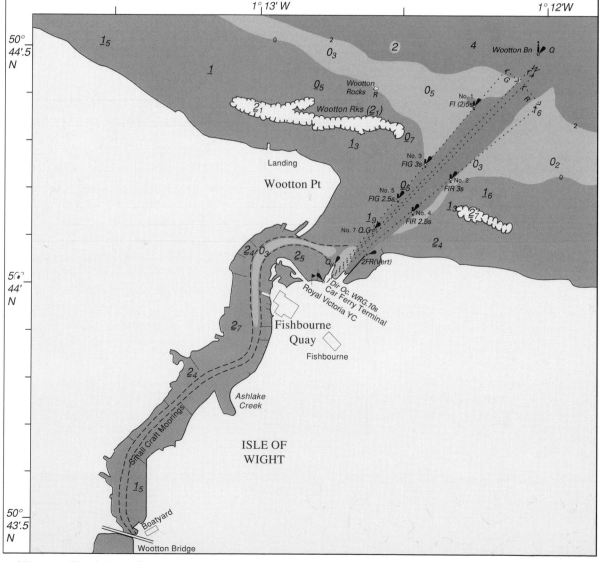

**Wootton Creek:** Soundings in metres.

The club has a dinghy hard, car park, changing-rooms and bar. Water, stores, bread, milk etc, can be obtained there and also meals. Nearby is the Fishbourne Inn. There is a launching site at HW. There is a boatyard at Fishbourne Quay, upstream from the yacht club.

In the upper reaches of the creek, the narrow channel is also occupied by moorings, but anchorage is possible on the mud for shoal draught craft or those which can dry out. At the top of the creek there is a public landing on the west side. On the east side close to the bridge there is a boatyard with marine engineers. At Wootton Village there are grocery shops, PO and laundrette. There is a garage up the hill to the west. EC Thursday. Good bus service to Ryde and Newport.

**Anchorage Outside:** Temporary anchorage is possible outside in moderate offshore winds, preferably to west of Wootton Beacon, and there is a popular anchorage at week-ends further to the west in Osborne Bay. A good position is off the HM Hard, half a mile west of Barton Point, but this is within the grounds of Osborne House and landing is not permitted. The anchorage is reasonably sheltered from W and S winds and the stream is weak.

### King's Quay Creek

This shallow trickle of water lies about a mile NW of Wootton, and looks from the sea to be larger than it is in reality. There is no neighbouring village, and the creek is equally difficult to approach either from land or sea, but, nevertheless, is attractive.

Years ago small yachts occasionally entered King's Quay and anchored among the exceptionally beautiful surroundings, but the channel is now unmarked. The creek itself is very narrow and winds between steep mud banks, but is worth exploring on a rising tide in a shallow draught craft or a dinghy.

At low water there is but a trickle in the 'Gutter', as it used to be called. The entrance is difficult to recognize from the north and is to the west of the little marshy valley which the gutter drains. A careful approach to the shore-line on a south westerly course should be made on a rising tide. There is now little to indicate the best course of approach and a preliminary recce by dinghy is recommended. At high water the marshes are mostly covered, the banks of the gutter will not be seen, and entry without prior knowledge very difficult. The entrance trends south-easterly, between two sandbanks which appear from seaward to overlap. Inside, the gutter winds through the marshes towards the woods, where it takes a sharp turn first north-west and then south, coming finally to a pool just below a decayed stone bridge and barrage. In this pool, approx. 1 m of water remains when the gutter has virtually dried out.

The banks are private property and the bottom of the creek is rented from the Crown by the Nature Conservancy Council which administers and wardens some 40 acres of the sea as a nature reserve. Landing is forbidden and the landing of dogs, in particular, would be very unwelcome.

# 10 Portsmouth Harbour

**Tidal Heights above datum:** MHWS 4.7 m MLWS 0.6 m MHWN 3.8 m MLWN 1.7 m. Flood 7 hours. Ebb 5 hours.
**Stream sets** to the NW outside at Spithead about −2 h 0 m Portsmouth and to the SE about +3 h 30 m Portsmouth, but the direction of the streams vary in the approach in relation to the local Portsmouth streams.
**Depths:** Ample at any state of the tide in the main ship channel.
**Principal Yacht Clubs:** R Albert YC, Royal Naval SA (and Service clubs), Hardway SC, Portsmouth SC, Gosport Cruising Club, Portsmouth Harbour Cruising Club.

PORTSMOUTH HAS BEEN closely linked with the Navy from the Middle Ages down to the Napoleonic wars and to present times. Nelson's *Victory* is open to visitors in the oldest dry dock in the world, and HMS *Warrior*, the *Mary Rose* and the naval museum all form an historic complex of maritime history. Although guided missile ships now replace the frigates of old, Portsmouth Harbour remains predominantly associated with the Royal Navy and comes under the jurisdiction of the Queen's Harbour Master.

The harbour covers an area of some 15 square miles which, apart from the dock area, consists of mud flats intersected by deeper creeks, of which Fareham and Portchester are the principal – see next chapter. Increasing use of the harbour has been made by yachtsmen in recent years, with Camper and Nicholson's marina near the entrance, Port Solent at the top of Porchester lake and Fareham Marina in Fareham Lake, and club or private yacht moorings in almost every accessible part where permission has been given to lay them. There is plenty of local racing, and at Southsea the Royal Albert YC provides the starting line for many ocean races and JOG events.

There is a 10 knot speed limit both inside Portsmouth Harbour and within half a mile of the shores of the Eastern Solent.

## The Approach and Entrance

Straightforward chartwork is all that is required for entry to Portsmouth, as the fairway is deep enough for an aircraft carrier and is well marked. Except at LW springs there is also enough water for most yachts on each side of the buoyed channel clear of the big ship fairway.

Approaching from the west it is usually quickest to follow the swashway used by the Portsmouth-Ryde ferries, which leads between the Hamilton Bank on its NW side and the Spit Bank on the SE side. The transit for this swashway is the conspicuous white Naval Memorial on the Southsea shore, about a quarter of a mile south-east of Clarence Pier, in line with the eastern edge of a conspicuous block of flats bearing 049°. Except at LW springs, it is not necessary to adhere exactly to the transit. When No 2 red can buoy is abeam, alter course to port up the fairway to the boat channel.

10.1  The white Naval Memorial in transit with the eastern edge of a distinctive block of flats on 049° leads up the swashway to the dredged channel. In this photo, taken from the north of the transit line, St Jude's Church spire can be seen in the background.

Round Tower    Tank

10.2.  The leading marks for the inner swashway are the western edge of the conspicuous tank in line with the western extremity of Round Tower at 029°.

Alternatively, with sufficient rise of tide and moderate weather, the inner swashway (not to be used by vessels 20 m and over in length) affords a short cut westward of Hamilton Bank in 0.3 m least water. The transit is the west side of a high conspicuous tank in line with the west extremity of Round Tower at 029°. However, there is only a difference of about 0.6 m in being on or off the correct transit. Local yachtsmen often merely follow the Haslar shore, keeping about 200 m off, with sufficient rise of tide, but this is not recommended in strong S to E winds, cross seas wash as back from the sea wall.

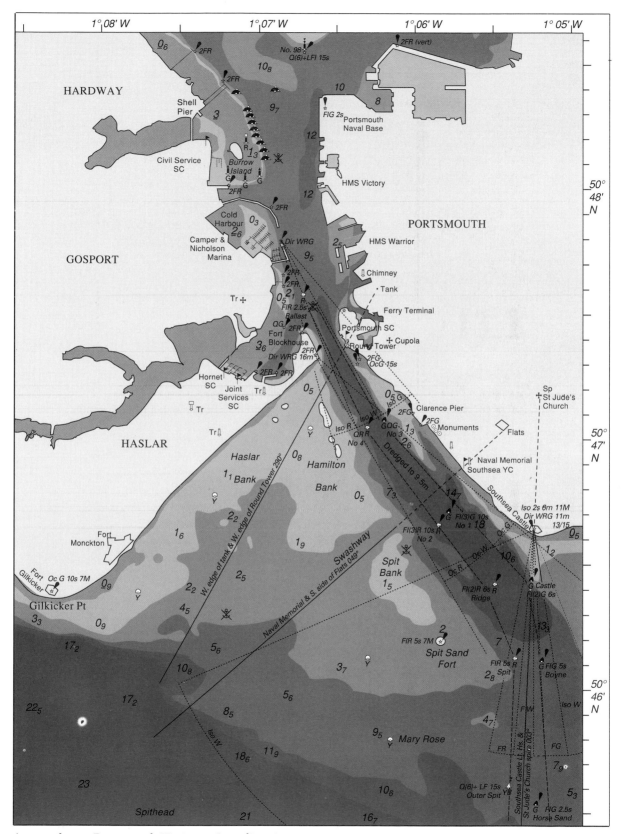

**Approaches to Portsmouth Harbour:** Soundings in metres.

From the eastward, vessels proceed off the Horse Sand Fort, up the buoyed channel towards Southsea Castle lighthouse in line with St Jude's Church spire at 003° and then alter course at Castle conical G buoy (*Fl (2) G 6s*) to follow the fairway to the entrance. If coming from Langstone or Chichester Harbours, distance can be saved by taking the gap in the submerged barrier about three quarters of a mile south of Southsea Beach. See Chapter 13. Note however that this barrier is a serious hazard on which yachts have been lost. There are no gaps through it other than the clearly marked boat passages.

## Small Boat Channel

There is a boat channel exclusively for vessels under 20 m long on the west side of the entrance. Such vessels must enter the harbour through the boat channel or close inshore on the east side of the entrance, but must leave only through the boat channel. Vessels with engines must use them between No 4 buoy and Ballast Buoy.

The flood tide starts at + 5 h 30 m Portsmouth and runs easy for 3 hours, and then strong for 4 hours; the ebb starts at + 15 m Portsmouth and runs easy for one hour increasing to maximum on the 3rd and 4th hour, attaining 5 knots at springs, and then eases. At the entrance of the harbour, however, owing to the mass of water running out of the creeks, the ebb continues to run hard for longer, and only slackens during the last 45 minutes. Yachtsmen are not advised to attempt entry at the 3rd and 4th hours of the ebb at springs, particularly when strong SE winds against a fast ebb will cause big seas just outside the entrance. When sailing against the stream it should be remembered that there is slacker water on either shore and sometimes a helpful eddy on the east side as far as Round Tower.

10.3.  No 4 Bar buoy, with its injunction 'Small craft use engine. Use small boat channel'.

10.5.  Ballast Buoy. The northern end of the small boat channel.

Numerous flag signals fly from the Semaphore Tower, Fort Blockhouse and Fort Gilkicker. These signals do not apply to vessels under 20 m, but yachtsmen should be aware that any signal containing a red flag with a white diagonal indicates a large vessel underway, from which they must keep clear.

The designated VHF channel for control of shipping by the Queen's Harbour Master is Channel 11. Vessels under 20 m do not need to advise of their arrival and should not use it to transmit, but a listening watch on approaching the entrance may give prior warning of shipping movements and enable avoiding action to be taken with ample time.

**Lights:** At night an incoming vessel should keep in the white sector of Southsea Castle light, *Iso 2s Dir W R G*, entering the ship fairway between the Outer Spit S Cardinal buoy *Q (6) + L Fl 15s* and the starboard hand Horse Sand buoy *Fl G 2.5s*. Thence proceed by chart in the well-marked channel. Fort Blockhouse on the port side of the entrance *Oc Dir W R G* will be seen next – incoming vessels should keep in the W sector – and finally the Harbour Entrance directional light *ISo 2s Dir W R G*, set on a concrete dolphin off the Camper and Nicholson Marina. The Small Boat Channel on the west of the entrance lies in the sector where R and W lights overlap.

## Moorings, Anchorage and Facilities

As stated earlier, the Queen's Harbour Master is vested with jurisdiction within Portsmouth Harbour and, indeed, outside from Cowes to the Nab. His office is within the Naval Dockyard, so it is best to contact him by telephone (0705 822351, ext. 23344), as moorings (including those allotted to clubs, yacht yards and licence holders) are under his supervision, which also extends to anchorages.

A visiting yachtsman will have to obtain the use of a mooring or marina berth at least temporarily. If possible, a booking should be made in advance, as few anchorages are available owing to prohibited areas, fairways for shipping and cables. The bottom is foul in many parts, so anchors should always have a trip line. The following yacht bases are listed in order of approach:

(a) **The Camber.** This is the commercial harbour of Portsmouth, situated just within the entrance on the east side. The Camber is used by the Isle of Wight car ferries and is usually packed with coasters, lighters and fishing boats, but does occasionally take visiting yachts.

(b) **Haslar Lake.** This creek lies on the west side just round Fort Blockhouse. The channel is deep and lies along the SW side between the jetty (where submarines berth) and an extensive mud flat on the NW side, marked by dolphins. It then turns west to Haslar bridge and the depth decreases to 1.8 m CD. Yachts with lowering masts can pass under the bridge into the continuation of the creek which is called Alverstoke Lake. The channel is marked by piles but is very shallow.

The Joint Services Sail Training Centre operates from a complex of pontoons at the south of Haslar Lake, near Haslar bridge, and there are many Service owned craft moored

10.4.   Looking SW into Haslar Lake, on the port hand just inside the entrance. There have been plans to build a new marina in the lake, but at the time of writing (1991) work had not started.

10.6.   View over Camper & Nicholson Marina to Portsmouth. HMS *Victory's* masts in the background.

there. There are also pontoons and moorings on the north-west side. There is no specific provision for visiting yachts. Anchorage is limited and the bottom is foul. All facilities at Gosport.

(c) **Gosport.** Camper & Nicholson's marina (Tel: 0705 524811) is situated above the ferry landing stage at Gosport, and has extensive facilities for yachts of all sizes. VHF watch is kept on Channels 37 and 80 – Callsign: 'CAMPER BASE'. Vessels are not allowed to berth on the marina breakwater pontoons.

Beyond Camper & Nicholson's marina lies the Gosport Borough Yacht Harbour in the Cold Harbour, enclosed by the same long, open-piled oil fuel jetty used by naval tankers. The Gosport Borough Yacht Harbour contains sets of double moorings, let on a long-term basis, but visitors are accommodated if there are temporary vacancies. Application should be made at the blue hut on the quay. Vessels may also make fast alongside the Town Quay, but this dries out and is never very pleasant. The adjacent scrubbing piles on the hard may be used on application. A Gosport marina is planned for the area of the mud bank west of Ballast buoy.

Besides the facilities already mentioned, there are shops of all kinds in the town including yacht chandlers (EC Wednesday, Gosport and Portsmouth; Thursday, Southsea) and also small restaurants and many pubs. Ferries to Portsmouth and buses to all parts. Landing steps (drying) near the ferry, and public launching site at Gosport Borough Yacht Harbour.

(d) **Weevil Lake and Forton Lake.** All available space in Weevil Lake is occupied by permanent moorings. The entrance lies north of the Cold Harbour immediately beyond the long jetty. This is left to port and a mud bank marked by piles lies on the starboard hand. The channel then turns sharply northward passing behind Burrow Island before bending to the west, where a wooden foot bridge separates it from Forton Lake. Depths in Weevil Lake are from 6.1 m at the entrance decreasing to 1.8 m. It dries out at CD near the foot bridge (which can be opened by appointment by Admiralty police in gate house). Forton Lake also dries out.

(e) **Hardway.** See Chart on page 94. This centre lies on the west side of the harbour about half a mile beyond the Shell Pier, in the entrance to Fareham Lake. The Hardway Sailing Club, (Tel: 0705 581875) is very active and hospitable. Every available space is now occupied by moorings off the club and to the north and south of it, on both sides of the channel. There is even an overflow of moorings for small cruising yachts in the entrance of Portchester, Bomb Ketch and Spider Lakes. The mooring area near the club is protected from westerly winds and there is a public hard and pontoons. The sailing club maintains a visitors' trot of fore and aft moorings off their pontoon, which has water laid on. There are so many other moorings that there is always the possibility of one being temporarily vacant, for which enquiry should be made at the club house. The club has a scrubbing grid, 1.8 m and launching site adjacent. Marine shop and fuels nearby. Other shops and pubs up the road facing the Hardway and a restaurant near Vosper's jetty. Short walk to bus stop for Gosport and Fareham.

(f) **Fareham and Portchester** – see next chapter.

10.7.   The Hardway SC pontoons. Two of the UHAF (Up Harbour Ammunition Facility) dolphins can be seen in the right background.

**Communications.** Express trains from Portsmouth Harbour Station and Town Station. Ferries to Ryde, IoW, adjacent Harbour Station, Car ferries to Wootton, IoW, from Camber. Buses from Portsmouth and Gosport ferry landings. Red Funnel ferries from Portsmouth Harbour Station to Cowes.

# 11 Fareham and Portchester Lakes

**High Water:** About +0 h 20 m Portsmouth.
**Tidal Heights:** Fareham above datum: MHWS 4.0 m MLWS 0.5 m MHWN 3.2 m MLWN 1.5 m.
**Local streams:** Shortly after HW the ebb runs for about 4 h 30 m, followed by 3 hours slack before 4 hours flood.
**Yacht Clubs:** Fareham Sailing and Motor Boat Club, Portchester SC, Portsmouth Harbour Cruising Club.

FAREHAM LAKE IS the NW arm and Portchester Lake is the NE arm from the junction with the main channel in Portsmouth Harbour. Both channels (which are 'lakes' only at high water) provide considerable reaches for sailing, though they are used principally by yachts of small or moderate size.

Fareham is situated round an ancient settlement at the ford where the present River Wallington joins the creek. It suffered greatly from the ravages of the Vikings, but survived and was mentioned in the Domesday Book, under the name of Fernham, when it was credited with one church and two mills. In recent years Fareham has grown a great deal and is a very busy small market town, with a great deal of light industry on its outskirts.

Historically, Portchester is of greater importance because of its castle, with walls dating from Roman times and enclosing a Norman church in an area of about nine acres. Throughout the Napoleonic wars many French and Spanish prisoners were confined there. The castle remains in an excellent state of preservation, dominated by the enormous keep, added by the Normans, from which a magnificent view of the yacht anchorage and the harbour is obtained.

Visitors should note the unusual numbering sequence of beacons and piles in Portsmouth Harbour and Fareham and Portchester Lakes. No 1 beacon is at the head of Haslar Lake near the harbour entrance. From there numbers lead up the west side of Fareham Lake, back down the eastern side, up the west side of Portchester Lake and again reverse direction at the northern end. By the time the eastern side of the main harbour is reached they are into treble figures. The main point to remember is that the more common 'even numbers to port, odd numbers to starboard' (or vice versa) does not apply in this area.

## Fareham Lake

This is the continuation of the main channel above Hardway, which has already been referred to, and the UHAF dolphins on the opposite side. It is a wide, deep water channel as far as Bedenham Pier and is clearly marked by red piles on the port hand and green piles to starboard. The piles should not be approached closely as some are on the mud banks which are very steep in most parts, but the edge is shoaling into the channel between No 48 and

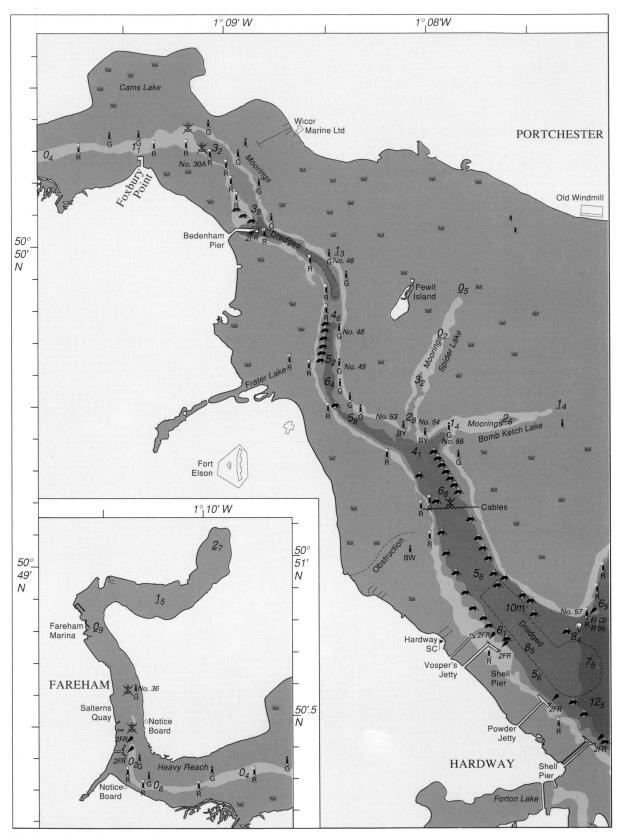

**Fareham Lake:** Soundings in metres.

11.1.    UHAF dolphins are to be left to starboard when sailing up Fareham Lake.

No 49 starboard hand pile. Avoid steering from one pile direct to the next as the mud sometimes edges into the channel between them, and do not take the bends too sharply. Bedenham Pier is Admiralty property and must not be approached within 12 m. A quarter mile beyond this pier on the opposite (starboard) side is the yacht yard of Wicor Marine Ltd, with long pier and pontoon off which there are many yacht moorings. Across from the pontoon is pile No 30A far up the mud which dries some 10 m on the channel side, and where many yachts go aground. The lake then takes a turn round Wicor Bend to the west into Heavy Reach where the channel becomes narrower and leads between extensive mud banks. This reach is marked by occasional piles, but these are well up on the mud. Pilotage is easiest at half tide, but can be confusing at high water when the mud flats are covered. The bottom is uneven, ranging from 2.4 m down to as little as 1.2 m in parts. Naval yacht moorings run west from the Naval pier on the south side and there are moorings for small yachts in shallower water on the north side.

At Power Station bend at the end of this reach, the Lake (now a creek) turns to north and passes under power cables with a clearance of 15.8 m at MHWS. The channel, which dries out at CD, then leads almost straight up to Fareham, edging to starboard a little under the trees about halfway up the reach. The mooring buoys here should be kept close under the port side, as they are on this side of the channel practically as far up as the quays.

A number of subsidiary creeks join Fareham Lake. Most of these dry out or are of little interest to visiting yachtsmen, but mention may be made of **Bomb Ketch Lake** and **Spider Lake**. As will be seen on the chart, these lie on the east side and enter Fareham Lake at the same point, the entrances being separated only by a spit of mud on which stands a S Cardinal pile (No 54). This should be left well to port and a G pile (No 55) to starboard if entering Bomb Ketch Lake. This creek leads east and carries variable depths. The upper pool has 3 m at MLWS, but other parts of the channel no more than 1.3 m. A few yachts are moored in the entrance, but anchorage at the eastern end is exposed at HW and the bottom is foul, besides being within the Tipner firing area. Spider Lake is entered between No 53 pile to port and No 54 pile to starboard, both S Cardinals. It leads about NNE for half a mile with a least depth of 1.8 m, rapidly shoaling to 0.7 m south-east of Peewit Island, and the upper reach is within the area of the Tipner rifle range. These lakes are far from facilities, are isolated and abound with birds and shellfish, as also does Peewit Island. Old

Naval cannon from Tipner range have been recovered at LWS. There are many private moorings in the main channel between Spider Lake and Wicor Marine.

**Frater Lake** on the west side of Fareham Lake leads to Bedenham Naval Quays where landing is prohibited. In **Cams Lake** there are two creeks leading to opposite corners of the bay. They dry out at LW.

### Moorings, Anchorage and Facilities

Anchorage out of the fairway is possible in Fareham Lake anywhere above Bedenham Pier, except in the prohibited areas west of the two notice boards and between Salterns Quay and No 36 pile, as shown on the chart, or in the vicinity of moorings. All need approval from the Queen's Harbour Master. It is necessary to use a trip line as the bottom is foul in many parts and a riding light is required because of shingle barges. Except at Hardway, referred to under Portsmouth, the best chance of obtaining the temporary use of a mooring is from the Wicor Marine Ltd (Tel: 0329 237112), who have many moorings for shoal draught yachts and a few yachts up to 1.8 m draught or more. Dry landing at pontoon at end of the long pier. Two slips and laying up and repairs undertaken. Chandlery, water and diesel, but far from shops.

Wicor Marine can launch from trailers craft of up to 7 tons displacement. Visiting yachts are welcome.

At Fareham small yachts have moorings. There is little water at LW springs but the bottom is soft mud and all except deep-keeled yachts will remain upright. Yachts of 1.8 m

11.2.   Fareham Marine pontoons at Lower Quay.

11.3.    Fareham Sailing and Motor Boat Club pontoon next to the Yacht Harbour.


11.4.    The approach to Port Solent Marina, looking north-east. The channel lies between the two lines of pile moorings on the left, with the final pair of beacons and marina reception pontoon beyond.

draught can proceed to the Lower Quay two hours either side of HW. Landing at pontoon at Fareham Sailing and Motor Boat Club, (Tel: 0329 280738). Water on application. Fareham Marine (Tel: 0329 832854) have pontoons at Lower Quay. Launching site at the public slipway nearby. There is an excellent shopping centre and pedestrian precinct not much more than a quarter of a mile's walk away and public conveniences nearby. A hotel and restaurants in the town. EC Wednesday. Market day Monday.

## Portchester Lake

Portchester Lake provides a good sailing area as the channel is wide and deep in its centre as far as Tipner Lake, but in parts there is only 2.7 to 3.0 m, and much less near the edges. In the reach up to Portchester Castle the bottom is even more irregular. Thus, although with local knowledge or with the aid of the large-scale No 2631 Admiralty Chart, 1.5 m CD may be found all the way to Port Solent Marina, a stranger may find as little as 0.6 to 1.2 m CD in some parts of the defined channel. It is well marked by numbered piles, red to port, green to starboard. However, some of these are well up on the mud or in shallow water, so they should not be approached closely nor (as in Fareham Lake) should a course be steered direct from one to the next at LW.

When approaching from Portsmouth Harbour, before coming to the UHAF dolphins, the red pile No 57 will be seen which marks the west side of the entrance to the Creek. The first reach, Long Reach, is not quite straight, although its general direction is NE. Off the entrance to Tipner Lake at the end of the reach on the east side, the main channel takes a turn to the NW. Here care should be taken as shallow water extends far beyond the No 67 pile on the port hand and there is a drying shoal on the starboard side between No 80 and No 79 piles. Here the best water is on the port hand off No 68 and No 69 piles, but beyond the latter the deepest water lies mid-channel, leading northwards past Portchester Castle.

Off Portchester Castle and above it, the channel to Port Solent Marina is narrow but dredged to 1.5 m CD. Red Pile No 72 (*Fl (3) R 10s*) and G Pile No 76 (*Fl G 5s*) are best passed in the eastern half of the channel to obtain maximum depth. Care should be taken north of No 73 red pile where a shallow patch protrudes into the channel from the west.

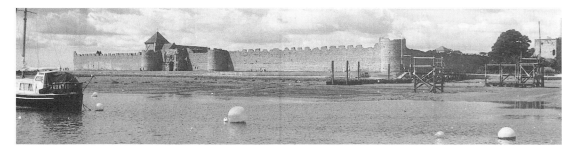

11.5.   Portchester Castle.

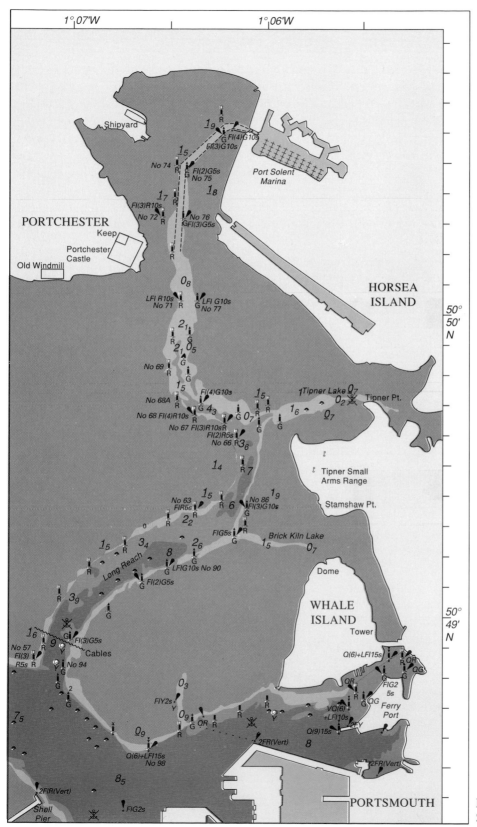

1°07'W  1°06'W

Shipyard

$1_9$
G Fl(4)G10s
Fl(3)G10s

Port Solent
Marina

$1_5$
No 74
R

Fl(2)G5s
G No 75

$1_8$

PORTCHESTER

Keep

$1_7$
Fl(3)R10s
No 72
R

No 76
GFl(3)G5s

Portchester
Castle

Old Windmill

HORSEA
ISLAND

$0_8$

50°
50'
N

LFl R10s
No 71
R

LFl G10s
No 77

$2_1$
G

$2_1$
$0_5$
No 69
G
R
G

$1_5$
No 68A
R

Fl(4)G10s
G $4_3$

$1_5$
R

$1$Tipner Lake $0_7$
$0_2$
Tipner Pt.

No 68 Fl(4)R10s R

$1_6$
G

$0_7$

No 67 Fl(3)R10s R
Fl(2)R5s
No 66 R $3_6$

$0_7$

$1_4$
R $7$

Tipner Small
Arms Range

Stamshaw Pt.

No 63
Fl R5s
$1_5$
R $6$

No 86
GFl(3)G10s
R

$1_9$

$2_2$
G

Fl G5s
G

Brick Kiln Lake

$1_5$

$0_7$

$1_5$
$3_4$
R

$2_6$
G

$1_5$

$8$
LFl G10s No 90
G

Long Reach

Dome

WHALE
ISLAND

$3_9$
R

Fl(2)G5s
G

Tower

50°
49'
N

$1_6$
Gi
$9$ Y
Fl(3)G5s

Q(6)+LFl15s
QR
G

QR
QG

No 57
Fl(3)
R5s R
Y
Y No 94
G

Cables

QR
R

FIG2
5s

$0_3$

Fl Y2s
Y

$0_9$
G QR
R R

QG

VQ(6)
+LFl10s
Y
QFY

Ferry
Port

Q(9)15s

$7_5$

$0_9$
R

$2$FR(Vert)

$8$

Q(6)+LFl15s
No 98

$8_5$

$2$FR(Vert)

Shell
Pier

FIG2s

PORTSMOUTH

**Portchester Lake:**
Soundings in metres

Pass No 73 some 20 to 30 m to the east and aim to pass midway between the next pair of piles, No 74 and No 75 (*Fl (2) G 5s*). The channel then turns northeast to the last two port and starboard piles where a turn to the east takes you to the lock at Port Solent Marina. The pontoon outside the lock is lit (*Fl (4) G 10s*).

**Port Solent** is a major 850 berth marina and housing complex close to the M27/M275 motorway junction north of Horsea Island. See Appendix 2 – Marinas and their Facilities.

**Tipner Lake.** This lake lies on the starboard side, where Portchester Lake turns westward about half a mile south of Horsea Island. It is marked by channel posts. The creek runs about easterly and passes through a prohibited anchorage before reaching Tipner Quays. Portsmouth Harbour Cruising Club has a landing at the drying concrete slip and water can be obtained at the club. On the port hand, opposite the quays, there is a small boat channel that links up with Langstone Harbour. This channel is not recommended for navigation as it is heavily silted up and not marked. After passing Tipner quays, a smaller channel branches off on the starboard side and leads along under the shore to the end of the promenade. At half tide, dinghies can land here, and it is only a short walk up the side-street to the buses which run to Portsmouth Guildhall.

**Danger area.** There is a danger area in Portchester Creek off Tipner Rifle Ranges which is shown on the chart and is defined by red notice boards. Limits are marked by pile Nos 70 and 78 to the north and pile Nos 63 and 87 to the south. Red flags are flown at the Butts when firing is in progress, normally all week, and yachts are requested to make passage through the area as quickly as possible.

**Moorings, Anchorage and Facilities**
The former anchorage, in rather poor holding ground in the channel south of the Castle, is now very limited as there are so many moorings that little room is left without encroaching upon the fairway. For the same reason, many of the yachts above the Castle are moored fore and aft so that they cannot swing into the fairway. Most of the moorings are licensed by the Portchester Sailing Club (Tel: 0705 376375) and let to their members. Application should be made to the duty officer of the club, which is helpful to visitors, to ascertain whether any moorings are temporarily vacant, but this cannot be counted on.

Landing at the north end of the Castle is made on the sailing club hard which has a concrete slip at the upper end. Yachts up to about 1.4 m draught with their own legs can be scrubbed here with a 3.6 m tide, and it also provides a launching site. The sailing club is in the Old Vicarage, alongside the hard. Water at tap near the Priory Church or on application at the club. There is a public car park and toilets about 100 yards from hard and the sailing club has its own car park. In the old village near the Castle is the Cormorant Inn and small shops, and three quarters of a mile up the road there are more shops, a PO, café, garage and bus stop. EC on Tuesday or for some shops Wednesday. The Castle is very well worth visiting.

# 12 Bembridge Harbour

**High Water** (Long): −0 h 5 m Portsmouth.
**Tidal Heights above datum:** Outside the harbour approximately as at Portsmouth. Within habour: MHWS 3.3 m MLWS 0.3 m MHWN 2.3 m MLWN 0.4 m.
**Stream sets** half a mile E of St Helens Fort weakly to S at +2 h 0 m Portsmouth, SE +4 h 0 m, S+6 h 0 m, NW −3 h 15 m, W −2 h 0 m, WSW +1 h 30 m.
**Depths:** A new approach channel was dredged in 1991, which carries 3 m for the first part of its length. However the centre section, some 0.2 miles E of St Helens Church, still dries 2 m or more at CD. Within harbour itself, there is said to be a minimum depth of 1 m in the channel from No 10 buoy to the marina. Access is restricted to 3 h either side of HW with approx 1.5 m draught.
**Yacht Clubs:** Bembridge SC, Brading Haven YC.

BEMBRIDGE HARBOUR OR Brading Haven, as it used to be known, is the most easterly of the Island harbours. It is a natural formation sheltered from the prevailing winds and with good facilities. The wide clean sands in the approach, fishing and shrimping and walks to the Foreland make Bembridge a good centre for the family yachtsman. In the days of sail St Helens Road provided an anchorage for the assembly of British fleets, and water casks were filled from a spring at Bembridge. The Road was the scene of the Spithead mutiny in 1797.

The disadvantage is that parts of the entrance channel and the harbour itself are so shallow that they severely restrict movement other than near HW. However, the Bembridge Harbour Improvements Company Limited are gradually improving the yachting amenities.

## The Approach and Entrance
The approach to Bembridge is via the yellow beacon (*Fl Y 2s*) situated about 300 m N of St Helens Fort (*Fl (3) 10s*). There is a tide gauge on the beacon which indicates the depth of water over the shallowest section of the channel, which is in the vicinity of Nos 6 and 8 buoys. The entrance to the channel is about 300 m to the W and is marked by two buoys, No 01 conical G to starboard and No 02 R can to port. They are not very big and are unlit. From here on the course to be taken is marked by green conical buoys with odd numbers to starboard and by red can buoys with even numbers to port. The approach channel is dredged from the outer buoys to a depth of 3 m below CD, this only extends to No 6 Buoy. The shallowest part is from No 6 to just beyond No 8 buoys. Their position is altered to suit the changing course of the channel and is only approximately shown on the chartlet. The channel becomes narrower and deeper as No 11 starboard hand buoy is approached. Ahead lies a pool where many club boats lie at moorings. To the east may be seen the Bembridge Sailing Club.

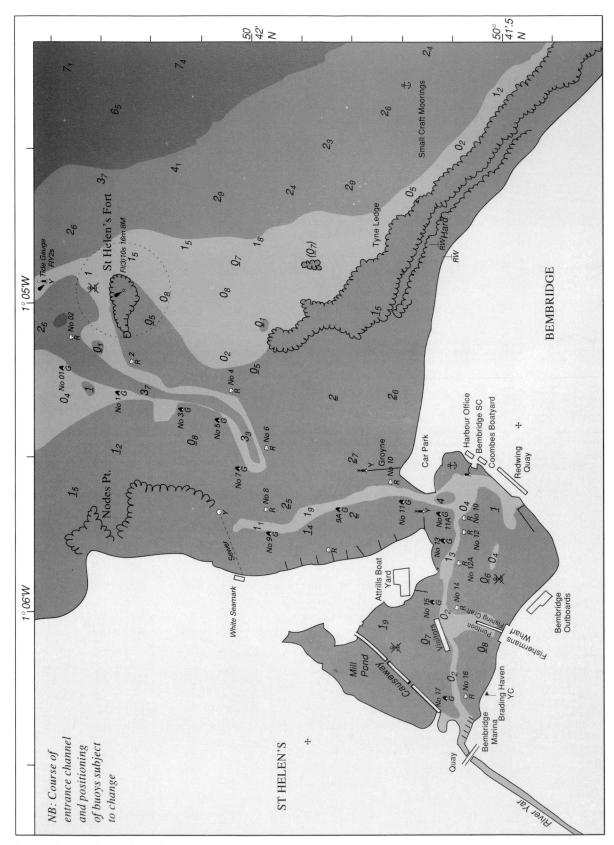

**Bembridge Harbour:** Soundings in metres.

12.1.   The Bembridge Ledge Buoy seen from the east.

12.2.   St Helens Fort to the left of Bembridge Harbour.

12.3.   St Helens Fort, now privately owned.

12.3.  No. 01 G conical buoy. The first of the
starboard hand marks.

12.4.  The second starboard hand mark is
No 1, seen here with St Helens Sea
Mark in the background.

The main channel to Bembridge Marina at St Helens Quay leads in a westerly direction and is marked on the starboard side by Nos 11A, 13, 15 and 17 G conical buoys and on the port side by Nos 10A, 12, 12A, 14 and 16 R can buoys.

The harbour is administered by the Bembridge Harbour Improvements Co Ltd. Their General Manager (in which the position of Harbour Master is vested) is Mr M H Coombes (Tel: 0983 872828).

**Lights:** Other than that on St Helens Fort (*Fl (3) 10s*), the only permanent light is the *Fl Y 2s* light on the beacon near the entrance.

### Anchorage, Moorings and Facilities

The best anchorage outside the harbour is at Under Tyne off the Bembridge SC starting line, half a mile to the east of the entrance. This position is well protected from winds from south to west, though exposed if the wind veers to NW and other directions. Anchor outside the permanent moorings in sufficient depth of water and buoy the anchor. The hard shown on the chart is more in the nature of a landing place between the rocks but at HW land on the beach whence follow the shore to Bembridge.

There are moorings for visitors alongside pontoons halfway up the harbour on the starboard side between Nos 15 and 17 buoys. A number of visitors' berths are available at the marina, where less than 1 m of water can be expected at LW, but below is soft mud and craft up to 1.8 m feet draught usually remain upright. Accommodation at the marina is very limited on Saturday nights and during the holiday period, so it is advisable to get in as early as possible on the tide leaving a margin for departure if necessary.

Craft that can take the ground are permitted to anchor fore-and-aft on the beach immediately to port on entering the inner harbour if there is space available. Anchoring elsewhere in the harbour is prohibited.

Drying moorings may be available from A A Coombes (Tel: 0983 872296) or from Attrill's Yard (Tel: 0983 872319).

The Brading Haven YC adjoins the Quay and temporary members are welcomed. There are small shops at St Helens a quarter of a mile up the hill. EC varies but PO Saturdays. Bembridge itself is nearly three quarters of a mile along the south harbour. Here there are hotels, restaurants and shops. EC Thursday.

Bembridge is an active racing centre with several yacht yards: Attrill's and Duver on the St Helens side of the harbour and Coombes, and Bembridge Boatyard Ltd on the south side. Chandlery at Coombes and yacht yards. Diesel fuel may be obtained from K. Stratton beside the marina and, subject to their own needs, from the jetties and pontoons off Attrill's and Duver's yards. Petrol can be obtained from a garage (closed Sunday) near Bembridge Church. Launching sites: concrete ramp near St Helens Church seamark (for about 3 hours either side of HW), and from sands and beaches, or by arrangement with yacht yards or at clubs by permission only. Buses to Ryde and all parts of the Island.

12.5.   Bembridge Marina visitors' pontoons.

# 13 Langstone Harbour

High Water: +0h 5m Portsmouth.

Tidal Heights above datum: Approx MHWS 4.8 m MLWS 0.6 m MHWN 3.9 m MLWN 1.8 m.

Stream sets in Hayling Bay rotary anti-clockwise 075° at about +5 h 45 m Portsmouth; 360° at −4 h 0 m; 315° at −2 h 0 m; 280° at HW; 260° at +1 h 0 m; 230° at +2 h 0 m; 160° at +2 h 30 m; 130° at +4 h 0 m; 110° at +5 h 30 m. Streams weak with maximum 0.9 knot HW to +1 h 0 m and 0.7 knot −5 h 0 m.

Depths: The depth of water on the inner Langstone Bar varies from time to time and has been about 1.8 m at CD, with as little as 0.6 m outside on the southern hook of the East Winner. Within the harbour there are reaches with 1.8 m and more – see chart.

Yachts Clubs: Locks SC, Tudor SC, Eastney Cruising Association.

LANGSTONE HAS ALWAYS been a somewhat neglected harbour and during the French wars it was much used as a retreat for privateers seeking to avoid pursuit in the English Channel. The inhabitants of Hayling Island were once well known for smuggling and wrecking. 'Mulberry Harbours' were made in Langstone Harbour in preparation for the assault on the beaches of Normandy in June 1944. The plan was for a harbour, built in sections, to be towed across and sunk on the French shore. There were several hundred of these concrete units made; one ran aground on the Sinah Sands, broke its back and remains as a monument to a remarkable achievement.

The days of privateers, smugglers and other colourful characters have passed but the lonely backwaters which they frequented still remain. There are creeks where the only sound comes from the seabirds, and reaches in the Langstone Channel where it is still possible to find room for cruising yachts to anchor in 1.8 m and over, though far from shore facilities. The harbour provides a good cruising area for dinghy sailing and there is plenty of active small boat racing.

The bar and the Winner sands, on which innumerable vessels have been driven ashore, have given the approach a bad reputation, but in normal summer weather and on the flood tide the entrance presents no particular problems. It is, in fact, easier than Chichester Harbour entrance.

## The Approach and Entrance

The approach from the Solent presents no difficulties. Hold a course past the Horse Sand Fort to clear the nearby shoal shown on the chart and the submerged barrier. Then steer NE to bring the Horse Sand Fort into line astern with Noman's Land Fort, whence keep on this transit steering 055°. This leads (in the direction of the prominent Royal Hotel almost midway on the front of Hayling Island) to Langstone RW Fairway buoy (*L Fl 10s*), distance about 2.3 miles. A BRB beacon (*Fl (2) 5s*) marking the dangerous Roway wreck will be left to port and an obstruction (2 m at CD) to starboard. Note: the wreck beacon is shown on

13.1. The Dolphin marking the south side of the main passage through the submerged barrier between Southsea and Horse Sand Fort.

13.2. The boat passage through the submerged barrier between Southsea and the Horse Sand Fort going west. South Parade just beyond the opening.

13.3. The wreck *BRB (Fl (2) 5s)* between Horse Sand Fort and Langstone Fairway buoy, less its topmark (see text).

13.4. Langstone Fairway buoy *RW (L Fl 10s)*.

the chart as having a topmark of two spheres vertical, but this is often missing. In poor visibility take care not to overstand the Langstone buoy.

If proceeding from Portsmouth a short cut may be taken through the gap in the barrier 0.8 miles south of the mainland shore. This passage is marked by a pile on an obstruction on the north side and a dolphin (Q R) on the south and carries 1.2 m CD. Then steer 079° for Langstone buoy heading midway between the conspicuous hotel and Eastoke Pt. The course leaves the wreck to starboard and leads just north of Langstone buoy. Alter course when it is sighted to leave it to port. There is also a second passage known as the 'Boat Passage' through the submerged barrier. This lies close inshore and is marked by beacons (see photograph on page 107); depth is only 0.9 m CD.

Approaching from the eastward, the hook-shaped extension of the East Winner extends over 1.5 miles from the shore, with depths as little as 0.6 m CD. At its extremity lies the YB Winner South cardinal buoy (unlit). These shoals (which frequently shift after gales and tend to lengthen) may be cleared in about 1.8 m CD by keeping Haslar hospital open southward of Southsea Castle, until the Fairway buoy comes into line with the east side of Langstone harbour entrance. Then steer for the buoy leaving it to port. Here the in-going stream begins + 5 h 40 m Portsmouth to the NE, gradually turning anti-clockwise to end WNW at high water. The maximum spring rate of 1.2 knots, direction 325° from − 2 h 0 m for an hour. The out-going begins to the south at + 1 h 20 m and attains maximum spring rate 2.1 knots S by E at + 3 h 0 m, ending easterly. The streams tend to follow the channel when the sands are uncovered and are stronger as the entrance, which is very deep, is approached. Here a spring rate of 3.5 knots is attained in the entrance on the flood (but there is an hour's slack at about half tide) and 4.5 knots (sometimes more) on the ebb which begins at + 0 h 25 m Portsmouth.

From the Fairway Buoy a course should be steered to the middle of the entrance between the sands, allowing for any athwartship tide. Alternatively, bring the beacons on the two

13.5. The conspicuous chimney on the west side of Langstone entrance and the two dolphins with beacons which give a useful transit.

dolphins on the west side of the entrance into line at about 344° and follow this transit, bearing to starboard about a quarter of a mile before reaching the entrance, when the channel is obvious.

The easiest time of approach in good weather is on the young flood before the East Winner (which is fairly steep-to) is covered so that the direction of the channel can be seen. At this state of the tide the East or West Winner affords some protection to the channel except during onshore winds. Nearer high tide, the East Winner can often be identified by the seas breaking on the sands: in bad weather they are covered by a mass of breaking water. During strong onshore winds and gales Langstone Harbour should not be approached as the seas break on the bar and in the shoal water far south of the Fairway buoy. The East Winner is a lee shore in south and SW winds; on the ebb tide under gale conditions it is particularly dangerous. Even in good weather entry on the ebb should be avoided, if possible owing to the strength of the stream in and near the entrance.

At the top of the narrows at the entrance pontoons for the ferries will be seen on either hand. Once past these the harbour widens out into a tidal lake more than two miles across, congested with sand and mud banks, but intersected with channels and small creeks.

**Gunnery Practice:** There is a rifle range at Eastney, with danger area SW towards the gap in the Barrier. The Fraser Gunnery Range, covering approaches to Langstone and Chichester harbours, is at Eastney Point SW of the chimney. **Danger Signals** displayed 30 minutes before and while firing. Large red flag above International Pendant 1 for **Area 1** (200 yards 120° to 200°). Above Pendant 2 for **Area 2** (6000 yards 120° to 155°). Above Pendant 3 for **Area 3** (12,500 yards 120° to 155°). Above Pendant 4 for **Area 4** (24,000 yards 126° to 146°). Areas 2, 3 and 4 use lethal ammunition. Signals are displayed from the range building, SW corner South Parade Pier, W side Langstone entrance, Harbour Master's Office and Selsey CG. A Naval Patrol boat, flying a red flag is stationed close to danger areas when areas 2, 3 and 4 are in use. Normal hours 1300–1530 Monday to Friday, but mornings may be used when weather on the previous days has been unsuitable.

**Lights:** After rounding the Fairway buoy *L Fl 10s*, the entrance can usually be seen at night against the lights on Portsdown Hill and there is a *Q R* light on the outer beacon at the west side of the entrance and *2 F R (vert)* marking the end of a jetty about 200 m beyond. A *Fl R* and then two separate *Fl 5 20s* lights lie on the port hand at the northern end of the entrance channel. Opposite, on the starboard hand, are *2 F G (vert)*. The approach channel to Langstone Marina, leading off to port just inside the entrance, is marked by solar powered lights on the tops of the most critical marker posts. Within the harbour there is a light on the port hand E Milton buoy *Fl (4) R 10s*, and opposite on the starboard hand NW Sinah buoy *Fl G 5s*. There is also a light *V Q R* in the Broom Channel at the entrance of Salterns Lake. In the Langstone Channel there is a lit buoy ALPHA *QR* and two lit beacons *Fl G 3s* and *Fl R 3s* near its head.

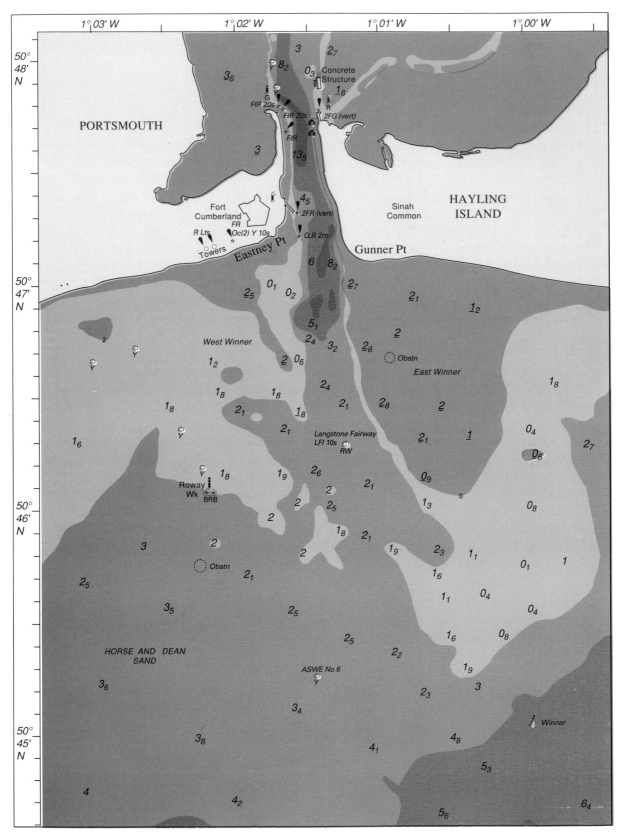

**Entrance to Langstone Harbour:** Soundings in metres.

## The Main Channel and Harbour

Within the entrance the main channel, which runs in a northerly direction, is wide and deep. On the west side it is joined at the entrance by Eastney Lake and on the east by Sinah Lake. Northward of these creeks the channel is very wide and there are many orange mooring buoys in deep water on the port side and an increasing number on the starboard hand in the vicinity of the concrete Mulberry grounded on the west of Sinah Sands. About a quarter of a mile beyond this is the previously mentioned green conical starboard hand NW Sinah buoy, and on the opposite side the red port hand E Milton buoy with a BRB beacon inshore of it. The deepest water is on the west side of the channel. There is plenty of water in the fairway marked for the dredgers between the two light buoys, though there is a small 0.3 m shoal just under a quarter of a mile south of the NW Sinah buoy, NW of the grounded Mulberry.

Beyond these buoys the Langstone Channel, which is deep for nearly two miles, branches off to the NE but the main channel continues northward for another half a mile before branching into the Broom Channel which continues NW to the road embankment north of Portsea Island.

Perches within the harbour have a high casualty rate due to oyster dredging and many are either missing altogether or are without their top-mark.

Owing to the number of moorings and the narrow fairway left for the gravel dredgers and ships proceeding to Kendall's Wharf, there is no room to anchor in the main channel. Anchorage is now only practicable in the Langstone Channel and Russell's Lake but shallow draught yachts can explore and find anchorages out of the fairways and in minor creeks not available to yachts of deeper draught.

## Moorings, Anchorage and Facilities

There are visitors' moorings for temporary use on the east side of the entrance, south of the notice board indicating where the cables cross. The position is exposed and very uncomfortable in high winds. In the case of SE winds of much strength, there is said to be a

13.6.   The Harbour Master's office (large building with flag-staff in front) and Ferry Boat Inn. Launching site between. One of the visitors' moorings in foreground.

13.7.   The stranded concrete 'Mulberry' marked as 'concrete structure' on some charts on the east side of the harbour. There is shallow water to the south of it and a shoal about 100 m to the north-west.

danger of these moorings dragging off the shelf and into the deep water of the channel; the ebb could then take one out to the Winner, mooring and all! It is best to go ashore to consult the Harbour Master who will advise whether any of the numerous moorings in the harbour are available for a longer stay and give any other information required. The Harbour Master, Captain P Hansen has his office nearby on the Hayling side of the ferry (Tel: 0705 463419). VHF watch on Channel 16, call sign 'LANGSTONE HARBOUR OFFICE': working channel 12.

**Water skiing** is permitted only with a licence from the Harbour Office and within certain specified areas. One such area is marked with yellow buoys and perches over the shoal sands either side of the Langstone Channel. There is a speed limit of 10 knots other than in the water skiing areas.

### Sinah Lake
Sinah Lake is on the Hayling Island side just within the entrance. All the best positions are occupied by moorings as is the Kench, the small bay on the south side, which dries out at low water.

It is best to enter Sinah Lake close to the ferry pontoon where there is 0.3 m CD whereas farther northward the sands dry out north of the red beacon. Care should be taken to avoid being set against the ferry pontoon where the stream is strong, especially on the ebb 2 hours after HW when it attains nearly 5 knots at springs. The channel runs at first NE and deepens to over 4 m north of the Kench. There is an inner bar which dries out as shown on the chart, and then a 0.4 mile reach to E and NE with depths ranging from 2.4 m down to 0.9 m CD at the eastern end. There are few marks to aid pilotage in the western part of Sinah Lake other than the yachts on moorings which show the trend of the channel, but some of these are shallow draught so keep close to the line of the larger yachts. The upper reaches are perched and lead to the Rod Rythe creek (which joins Sinah Lake to the Langstone Channel) and is also marked by perches. This provides a short cut which can be used by dinghies and shallow craft and is stated locally to be navigable by yachts at about half tide.

There is no room available in Sinah Lake for anchoring, so the visiting yachtsman should apply to the Harbour Master at Ferry Point for the use of a vacant mooring if any is available.

At Sinah there is the Ferry Boat Inn, and a café which supplies stores in summer. Water point behind the Inn, or from premises opposite who also supply fuel. Harbour Master's office and workshop adjacent. Launching site on slip. Car park nearby. Bus service to Hayling Village in summer, where there are hotels, shops and PO. EC Wednesday. Frequent ferries in daylight hours to Eastney, thence summer bus service to Southsea. Fuel and water from the Harbour Board premises.

### Eastney Lake (or the Locks) and Langstone Marina

This shallow lake lies just inside the entrance of Langstone Harbour on the west side, opposite Sinah Lake. To enter the lake, which also gives access to Langstone Marina, an incoming vessel should pass between the Ferry Pontoon and the first Royal Marine mooring buoy. Then the buoy should be kept straight on her stern, and course steered slightly south of west in the passage between the craft moored on each side of the creek. This creek should be approached with caution as the channel is narrow and is congested with moorings for small craft. The approach channel to the marina is marked by posts and carries a minimum of 1 m at CD, increasing to 2.5 m at the marina holding pontoon. Entry to the marina is controlled by an automatic cill, open approximately three hours either side of HW. All the usual facilities available – see Appendix 2: Marinas and their Facilities. There is another channel running south just inside the Ferry point, at the entrance to Eastney Lake, but it is very shallow.

The Locks Sailing Club is situated at Milton Locks on the north side of Eastney Lake; it is an active club and holds numerous dinghy races during the summer. There is a hard just north of the Locks, and a general stores up the road. EC Wednesday. Easy connections with Southsea and Portsmouth. Launching site at end of road near Ferry Pontoon.

Milton or Velder Lake is the next shallow creek north of Eastney Lake on the west side of the main channel, but is of little significance as it leads only to an area of reclaimed land.

### Broom Channel

This continuation of the main channel in a NW direction to Hillsea is used by ballast dredgers as far as Kendall's Wharf. It is comparatively narrow but carries 2.1 m of water

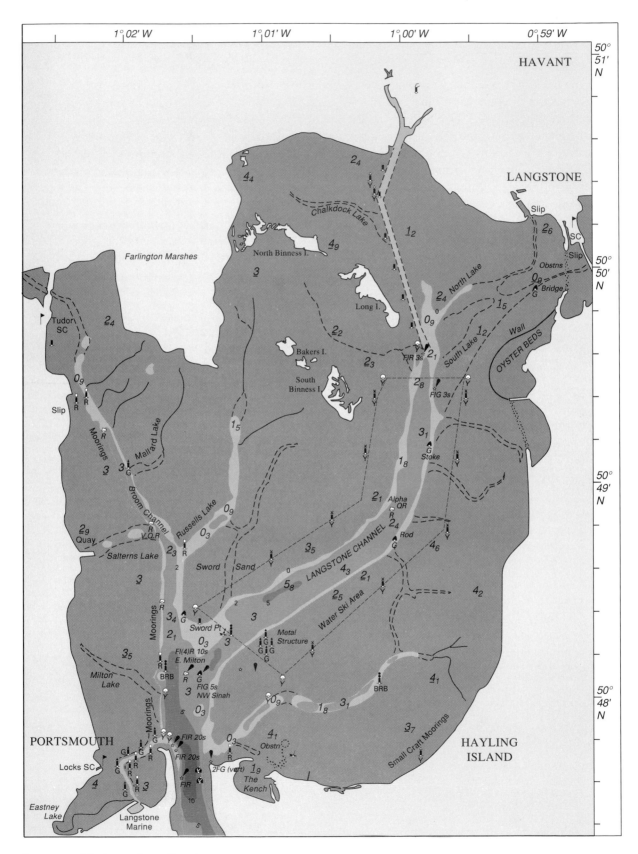

**Langstone Harbour:** Soundings in metres.

for the first half mile, though it shoals quickly a quarter of a mile south of Kendall's Wharf and dries out at chart datum just beyond. It is marked by perches on the mud on either side and three buoys. The Tudor Sailing Club is situated at the northern end of this channel near the road bridge and has many moorings for shallow draught craft. Half a mile to the south is the Portsmouth Schools Sailing Centre. There is no room for anchoring in the deeper part of Broom Channel below Kendall's Wharf as the fairway is used by the ballast dredgers. Apply to the Tudor SC (Tel: 0705 662002) to ascertain whether a visitor's mooring is available.

**Russell's Lake** joins Broom Channel on the east side and runs between mud flats to Farlington Marshes. It is only 0.3 m CD in the entrance but has deeper pools with from 1.5 m to 3.0 m. It is marked by occasional perches. The pools provide quiet, though rather remote, anchorages.

13.9.   East Milton buoy (*Fl (4) R 10s*) looking south-west. Beacon *BRB* behind.

13.10.   The R SALTERNS buoy (*V Q R*) at the entrance to Salterns Lake. Great Salterns Quay in the background.

13.11.   Kendall's Wharf near the head of Broom Channel.

**Saltern's Lake** lies on the west side of the Broom Channel. It has a red buoy (*V Q R*) at the entrance and perches mark the channel. It is no longer used by ballast dredgers and is largely filled by yacht moorings.

**Langstone Channel**

The entrance of this channel lies northward of the Sinah sands and the NW Sinah green conical light buoy (*Fl G 5s*). There is a middle ground in the entrance with as little as 0.3 m CD and a wreck marked by a BRB beacon with two black spheres. The easiest entry is south of this shoal, approaching from the NW Sinah buoy and treating the wreck beacon and four moored Admiralty rafts as port hand marks. Leave to starboard the metal structures which are well up on Sinah sands. The channel is wide and deep, ranging from 5.5 to 2.7 m for the first mile. It runs in a NE direction and is marked by occasional perches. The yellow buoys are water skiing marks, sometimes in shallow water; they may help to indicate the general direction of the channel. About a mile from the entrance there is a red

13.12. The first of the four Admiralty rafts in Langstone Channel, looking back to the wreck beacon *BRB*.

13.13. The R buoy ALPHA (*Q R*) about a mile up the Langstone Channel.

13.14. The unlit G buoy ROD marks the east side of the channel opposite Alpha.

13.15. The small G buoy BRIDGE at the head of South Lake.

13.16. Havant Quay at the north end of the Langstone Channel.

lit buoy ALPHA (*Q R*) and an accompanying unlit starboard hand green buoy ROD. The channel turns north to another green starboard buoy STOKE and two lit beacons *Fl R 3s* and *Fl G 3s* that mark the dredged channel to Havant Quay.

North Lake and South Lake both dry out and lead easterly through the gap in the former railway bridge to Hayling road bridge. North Lake is the better marked of the two and navigable with sufficient rise of tide if proceeding to Chichester Harbour. A green buoy BRIDGE provides a starboard mark. But although the charts indicate 'marked by perches', they should not be relied upon. The road bridge can only be passed under by craft without masts as there is no more than 2.1 m clearance below it at high water springs and the stream is strong. The span of the bridge with the best water under it is marked on the pile on the north side with a black diamond on a white background with black bands below it and by a black triangle on the south side. For Langstone village see Chichester Harbour.

There is plenty of room to anchor in Langstone Channel, which is quiet except in strong winds against the tide or when water skiing is in progress. The best holding ground is on the north side, little more than a mile from the Locks SC which is not far by dinghy with outboard engine in ordinary weather. However, it is important to anchor well clear of the channel, as the dredgers that ply to Havant Quay have, it is said, scant respect for anchored yachts.

13.17. Hayling Island road bridge separates Langstone and Chichester harbours.

# 14 Chichester Harbour

**High Water:** At entrance +0 h 5 m Portsmouth.
**Tidal Heights above datum:** Entrance MHWS 4.9 m MLWS 0.7 m MHWN 3.9 m MLWN 1.8 m.
**Stream sets** to westward 2.1 miles S of Cakeham Tower at 1 knot maximum −2 h 0 m Portsmouth. Begins about NW rotating anti-clockwise to finish S, and easterly stream begins +5 h 0 m Portsmouth. For Hayling Bay see Langstone Harbour.
**Depths:** Bar dredged to 1.5 m CD giving over 2 m at MLWS, but depths and sands vary from time to time. Channel at entrance very deep. Inner bar NE of the NW Winner Buoy 1.5 to 2.1 m. In Chichester Channel depths vary from 2.7 m upwards as far as Itchenor.
**Yacht Clubs:** Birdham YC, Bosham SC, Chichester YC, Dell Quay SC, Hayling Island SC, Itchenor SC, Langstone SC, Mengham Rythe SC, Thorney Island SC (RAF), West Wittering SC.

CHICHESTER IS ONE of the largest and most concentrated yachting centres in the South of England. This is not surprising as it provides a cruising area in itself, with several miles of sheltered water in its four main channels: Emsworth, Thorney, Bosham and Chichester. Besides this, all the creeks and harbours of the Solent are within easy reach and it is a good point for departure to France or more extended cruises. It is also a great centre for dinghy and other racing. Within the harbour there is a speed limit of 8 knots for yachts under power.

Historically, the harbour has associations deeply rooted in the past for it was known to Roman, Saxon and Dane. At one time there was a monastery in the village of Bosham and the largest bell was seized and carried away by the Danes on one of their numerous raids. Legend has it that no sooner had the raiders departed than the monks returned to the belfry and began a peal. The missing note came ringing over the water from the Danish vessel, over a mile away in Bosham Deep; then the bottom of the raiders' ship opened, the bell sank, and the planks of their vessel closed together again. According to the legend, the bell could only be recovered by a team of pure white heifers. Today, a replica of the bell is seen on the burgees of members of the Bosham Sailing Club in all parts of the harbour, but, to date, the team of white heifers has remained lacking.

## The Approach, Bar and Entrance

There are extensive shoals off the entrance to Chichester, and large parts dry out at low water. On the west side there are the West Pole sands, which have extended south beyond the Bar Beacon (see chartlet). On the east side, the Middle Pole and the East Pole sands extend nearly 1.5 miles off the shore. A depth of 2 m at MLWS can be expected at the bar, but after gales the bottom can vary by 0.75 m either way. An incoming yacht must wait for sufficient rise of tide to cross the bar with an adequate factor of safety, especially in rough

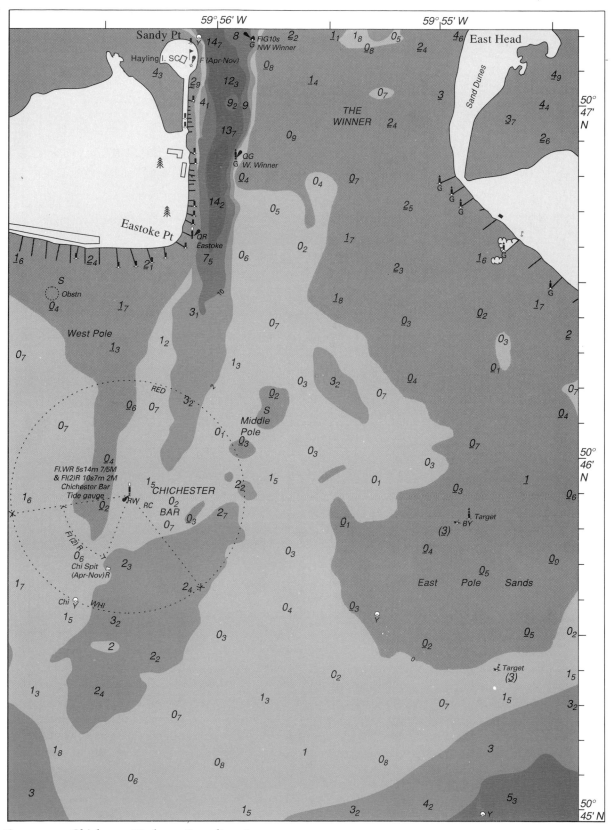

**Entrance to Chichester Harbour:** Soundings in metres.

14.1.   Chichester bar beacon.

14.2.   The small R can buoy some 800 m south of the Bar Beacon (see text).

14.3.   West Winner beacon (Q G) and tide gauge.

weather or a swell. In normal weather with reasonable visibility, there is no difficulty about approach and entry after half flood, but the ebb attains a spring rate of well over 5 knots at the entrance. A yacht under sail cannot make headway against this unless she has a commanding wind or auxiliary power. In common with all shoaling lee shores, extra care should be taken if approaching with onshore winds or swell. The approach is dangerous in thick weather and extremely so with strong or gale force southerly winds against an ebb tide, when an alternative destination should be chosen.

When approaching from east or west keep well offshore (according to the height of the tide and weather conditions) until the clump of trees at Eastoke Point (see photograph) on the west side of the entrance and Chichester Bar Beacon (*Fl W R 5s*) have been identified. Approach can then be made from due south. Near LW, deep draught vessels approaching from the west and south-east should steer courses to arrive at a point at least one mile south of Chichester Bar Beacon before altering course to the northward. An unlit red can buoy bearing 187°, about a quarter of a mile from the Bar Beacon encourages mariners to give the West Pole Tail a wide berth. Leave the Bar Beacon close to port and shape a course to pass midway between Eastoke and West Winner Beacons. On this course a minimum depth of water of 1.4 m at CD will be found just abreast the Chichester Bar Beacon. Shallow patches exist to the east and west of the approach course. The Chichester Bar

14.4.   Eastoke Point and conspicuous trees.

Beacon bears a tide gauge which indicates the depth of water above CD, thus if it reads 1.0 metres there will be a depth of 2.4 metres 200 m to the east of it. When the bar has been crossed, the depths slowly increase to 2.7 m when half a mile off the entrance and at least a depth of 9.0 m in the entrance.

As the entrance is approached, it will be seen that there are three groynes, with drum-topped beacons on their seaward ends which must be left well to port, as they dry 1.5 m. A fourth has the Eastoke Beacon (*Q R*) on it. This beacon should be left 100/200 m to port, and beyond it are three more beacons, all to be left to port as the yacht comes into the entrance.

In the entrance itself the deepest water lies in the centre of the channel but there is also plenty of water on the west side as the beach is fairly steep-to. The whole of the area to the east is choked by a big shingle bank, the Winner, extending over half a mile from the eastern shore, and the channel lies between the shore and the West Winner Beacon (*Q G*) which is to be left to starboard. Continuing along the western shore, Hayling Island Sailing Club, standing on Sandy Point at the northern end, will be left to port, with the green conical NW Winner buoy (*FL G 10s*) on the opposite side of the channel. Leading off to port immediately north of Sandy Point is the approach channel to Sparkes Yacht Harbour.

**Lights:** There is a *Fl WR 5s 14m + Fl (2) R 10s 7m* light on the Chichester Bar Beacon. Keep well offshore until in the 120° white sector of this light. The beacon on the groyne carries a *Q R* light, while that on the W Winner Beacon shows *Q G*. These are followed by the NW Winner buoy showing *Fl G 10s* which is left to starboard, then Fishery buoy's *Q (6) + LFl 15s* south cardinal light will be seen.

The Emsworth channel is well lit with NW Pilsey buoy (*Fl G 5s*), Verner beacon (*Fl R 10s*), Marker beacon (*Fl (2) G 10s*) and the two beacons, NE Hayling (*Fl (2) R 10s*) and

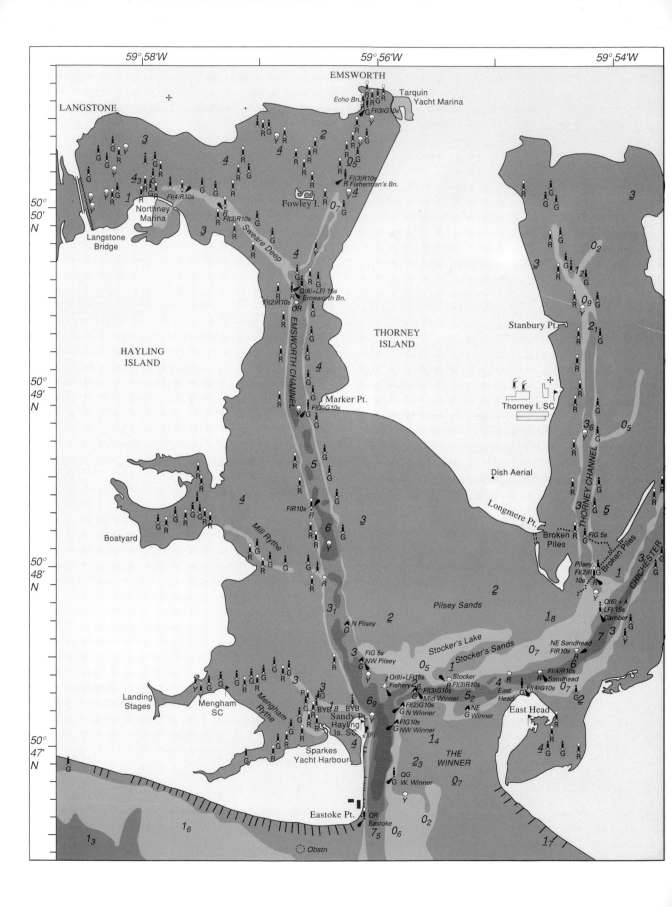

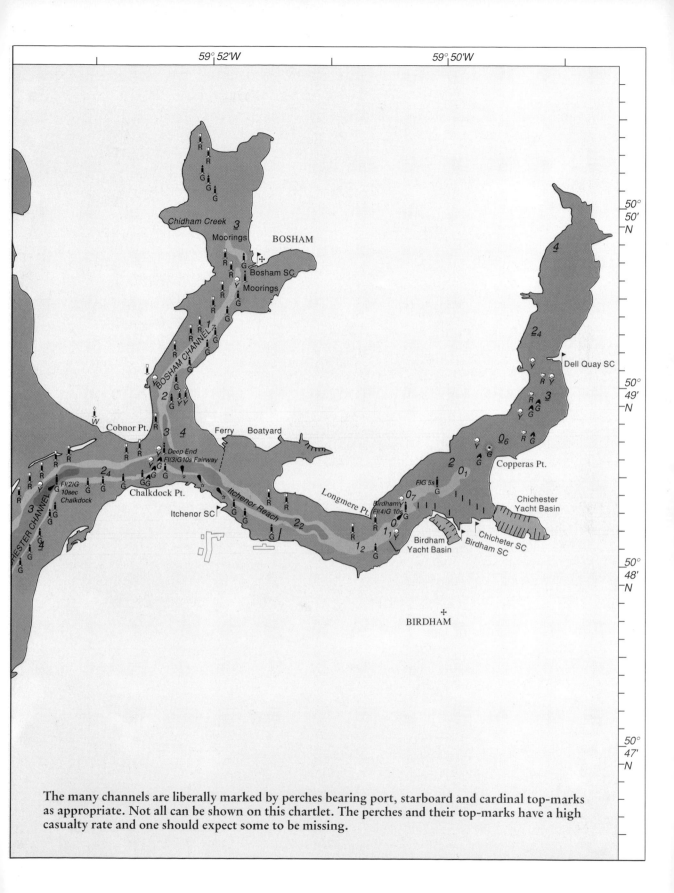

The many channels are liberally marked by perches bearing port, starboard and cardinal top-marks as appropriate. Not all can be shown on this chartlet. The perches and their top-marks have a high casualty rate and one should expect some to be missing.

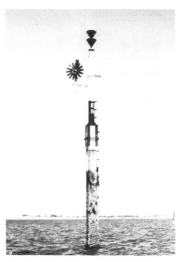

14.5.  Fishery south cardinal
buoy (*Q (6) + L Fl 15s*).

14.7.  Camber Beacon.

14.8.  Roman Transit.

Emsworth beacon (*Q (6) + L Fl 15s*). Up Sweare Deep the Sweare Deep beacon shows *Fl (3) R 10s* and the Northney beacon at the entrance to the Northney Marina channel *Fl (4) R 10s*. The marina itself is well lit by pontoon lights and will be quite apparent. The northerly channel to Emsworth and the Tarquin Yacht Harbour is lit by Fisherman's beacon (*Fl (3) R 10s*) and beyond, Echo beacon (*Fl (3) G 10s*).

The Chichester channel is similarly well lit as far as Itchenor: The N Winner (*Fl (2) G 10s*), Mid Winner (*Fl (3) G 10s*) buoys and the East Head beacon (*Fl (4) G 10s*) mark the starboard side of the channel, while Stocker (*Fl (3) R 10s*), Sandhead (*Fl (4) R 10s*) and NE Sandhead (*Fl R 10s*) buoys mark the port hand and northerly side. From here will be seen the Camber beacon with the south cardinal light (*Q (6) + L Fl 15s*) marking the division of the Thorney and Chichester channels.

In the Thorney channel the Pilsey Island beacon (*Gp Fl (2) R 10s*) marks the port side of the gap in the first line of broken piles and a further beacon (*Fl G 5s*) marks the starboard side of the gap in the second line of broken piles.

The Chichester channel continues lit by the Chalkdock beacon (*Gp Fl (2) G 10s*) and Fairway buoy (*Gp Fl (3) G 10s*). The Harbour Master's pontoon at Itchenor is lit by 2 *FG* (vert). After this there are only the Birdham beacon (*Gp Fl (4) G 10s*) and the CYB beacon (*Fl G 5s*) that mark the channels to Birdham Yacht Basin and Chichester Yacht Basin.

## The Chichester Channel

The directions will have brought the yacht within the entrance off Sandy Point and course altered to starboard to pass between the N Winner buoy (starboard) and the Fishery buoy to port. There is something in the nature of an inner bar extending from the N Winner

14.6    In the distance Stoke Clump is over the middle of the trees with the Roman Transit beacon in transit at 032°.

buoy to the west end of the drying part of the Stocker's Sand. The least water is 2.1 m. The course then becomes almost due east and the channel soon deepens. It leads between the Stocker's Sand on the north side – steep-to and dries 1.8 m in parts – and the Winner Sand on the south. The former is marked by the red can Stocker (*Fl (3) R 10s*) and Copyhold port hand buoys and the latter by the Mid-Winner (*Fl (3) G 10s*) and NE Winner starboard hand green conical buoys. After passing between the Copyhold and NE Winner buoys, the channel bears to the NE, leaving the sandy promontory of East Head to starboard and the Sandhead red can buoy (*Fl (4) R 10s*) to port.

After passing the latter buoy a very conspicuous distant clump of trees called Stoke Clump will be seen (except in hazy weather) to the NE and in the nearer distance, about 1.5 miles away, will be seen a wooded shore. The correct course up the next reach of Chichester Channel is held by keeping Stoke Clump over the middle of the trees on the wooded shore and with a white diamond beacon on the foreshore about a quarter of a mile west of Cobnor point at 032° (see photograph). If Stoke Clump is obscured there is Roman Transit Beacon in foreground which can be used. It is best to steer on a transit because some of the perches on the starboard hand in this reach are far up on the mud, which extends over a quarter of a mile from the shore in some places and is covered near high water, creating a hazard on which many yachts run aground. The Transit leads close to the Camber, South Cardinal beacon (*Q (6) + L Fl 15s*) situated on the NE side of the entrance to the Thorney Channel. This should be left to port and, continuing up the main channel, the broken piles and stumps of the old proposed embankment will lie well up on the mud beyond the port hand perches the whole way to Cobnor.

Towards the end of this reach at the Chalkdock beacon (*Fl (2) G 10s*) the channel bears to the east and the beacon is rounded leaving it on the starboard hand, as the mud extends nearly half a mile from the shore with two measured distance beacons with triangle tops high up on it. The channel then runs south of Cobnor Point leaving the Deep End beacon and the entrance to Bosham Channel to port and passing the green conical Fairway buoy (*Fl (3) G 10s*) on either side as it is in deep water. South of the buoy is another pair of measured distance beacons, half a mile from the first pair. The channel turns about ESE into the Itchenor Reach, and is wide and well marked. This reach leads past Itchenor, a charming village of red-stoned houses and cottages on the south side. The fairway is crowded by lines of yachts on moorings, but a passage is left between them.

The channel continues for nearly a mile beyond Itchenor before bending round Longmore Point (off which the channel is marked by several red can perches) to a north and then more north-easterly direction. The reach beyond this is not nearly so well marked and can only be navigated with sufficient rise of tide. As far as the entrance to Birdham Pool there is 0.3 m CD, but the mud extends a long way from the southern shore and the best water is on the northern side.

The creek leading to Birdham Pool and Chichester Canal is entered by leaving Birdham Beacon (*Fl (4) G 10s*) to port and then following a series of starboard hand piles. The dredged channel to the entrance of Chichester Yacht Basin is about a quarter of a mile beyond Birdham Beacon; it is marked on the starboard hand by six green piles with triangle tops. Do not steer direct from Birdham beacon to the CYB beacon as this course crosses drying mud on the starboard hand. Steer to leave both Birdham and CYB beacons about 100 m to starboard and do not alter course to enter the dredged channel until two leading marks, BW perches with crosses on the shore on the port hand, come into line. Then follow their transit to the CYB beacon and follow the dredged channel.

If continuing up the Chichester Channel to Dell Quay, leave the transit when the CYB beacon is about 100 m distant and steer for the green buoy off Copperas Point, leaving it to starboard.

The channel dries only 0.3 m but is narrow and winding for the first quarter of a mile NE of the pile, so a stranger may not find the best water. Beyond Copperas Point the channel is shallower, drying about 1.2 m at CD, thus having no more than 0.6 m at LW neaps. In the reach between Copperas Point and Dell Quay there are buoys to mark the narrow winding course. The first and last are red port hand can buoys, and the two between green starboard hand barrels. All are now of GRP. After passing the last buoy the best water lies towards the end of the quay.

### Thorney Channel

In this channel there is 1.8 m and more in most parts to within a quarter of a mile of the junction of the two creeks at its head. The entrance lies to the south-west of the South Cardinal Camber Beacon, which lies about 100 m to starboard when entering the channel. The area in the vicinity northward of the buoy has been getting shallower of recent years, so do not try short cuts. An orange racing buoy is often moored near the Camber beacon.

14.9. (Left) Port hand beacon off Pilsey. (Right) Two beacons off Longmere Point marking lines of broken piles on each side of the Thorney Channel.

On the SE side of Pilsey Island on the port hand is a line of broken piles marked near its end by a red beacon which should be left close to port. On the opposite side of the channel there is the end of the similar line of broken piles to Cobnor, previously referred to. At the end of this line of piles is a dangerous shoal which dries out 1.5 m and on which there is usually (but not always) a green perch which must be left to starboard. About 400 m farther up the channel, east of Longmere Point, there are similar lines of broken piles on each side. The narrow fairway between them is marked by an iron beacon with red can top on the port hand side and a green beacon with triangle top to starboard. From here the channel runs northward and is marked by occasional perches, but note the 1.2 m shoal on the E side off the entrance to Crake Rythe, SE of West Thorney.

At West Thorney there is the Thorney Island SC, and a hard. A number of yachts and small craft lie on moorings in this part of the channel. Thorney Channel divides at its end into two little creeks which run up to Nutbourne and Prinstead villages. Larger vessels should not proceed beyond the junction without local knowledge.

On Thorney Island there is a small village with a church, the sailing club, and a farm, but no shops nor facilities. Most of Thorney Island is Army property and there is no access by road from the mainland to the hard, club and church, except by permission. There is plenty of room to anchor in Thorney Channel, and shallow draught boats and dinghies can go up on the tide to Prinstead where there is a boatyard.

14.10.   Deep End beacon at the entrance to Bosham channel.

**Pilsey Island** is uninhabited, and is little more than a semi-circular sea wall. For conservation reasons, landing is restricted to the beach adjacent to the anchorage (east of the island) during daylight hours from 1st April to 31st October.

### Bosham Channel

One of the most picturesque parts of Chichester Harbour is at Bosham, and the channel is easy to navigate though there are many yachts moored there, leaving a rather narrow fairway. The entrance of the creek runs in a northerly direction out of the main Chichester Channel half a mile west of Itchenor. The South Cardinal Deep End beacon (unlit) marks the east side of the entrance and it is best to keep fairly near this, giving Cobnor Point on the port hand a wide berth. The first reach runs north and the channel is clearly marked by the numerous moorings.

The creek is 1.8 m or more deep until within about a quarter of a mile from the village, when it shallows and almost dries out off Bosham Quay. Beyond this, Chidham hard, on the west side, extends three-quarters of the way across the creek and is mostly submerged at high tide; a post marks its eastern extremity and there is also a hard on the Bosham side. Further north there is a narrow channel which at high water forms quite a wide lake.

### Moorings, Anchorages and Facilities

The Harbour Master (Capt J A Whitney) controls all the moorings which are rented to yacht owners and for which there is a waiting list. His office is at Itchenor Hard, facing the river (Tel: 0243 512301) where there is a Port Operation and Information Service. VHF

14.11.   Itchenor hard and the Harbour Master's pontoon. Visitors' mooring in the foreground.

watch is kept on Channels 16 and 14, 0900–1300 and 1400–1730 on week days: 0900–1300 only on Saturdays during the season. Call CHICHESTER on Channel 14.

There are 6 white visitors moorings at Itchenor; each will take six craft rafted up.

At **Birdham Pool** there is access to the approach channel about 3 hours either side of HW depending on draught, and the lock gates can be opened 2 hours each side of high water with free flow in the lock for 1 hour at springs. At the **Chichester Yacht Basin**, about a quarter of a mile farther on, the river outside dries at CD, but in the channel dredged through the mud to the entrance there is about 1 m LW on an ordinary spring tide and more at LW neaps. Yachts may secure to the beacon piles or to piles either side of the lock gates while waiting entry. The lock gates to the basin can be opened at any time and there is free flow for 1 hour springs or 4 to 5 hours neaps. Lock control is indicated by boards: red (wait), green (enter) by day; at night the boards are floodlit and only when there is free flow a Q amber light is exhibited on top of the lock tower. See Appendix 2 for facilities.

**Anchorages.** West of Fairway buoy on the south side of the channel; east of Pilsey Island; north of East Head; and north of Sandy Point, at the entrance to Emsworth Channel.

**The Itchenor Ferry.** This useful service operates from the Itchenor jetty to Bosham Quay; Bosham Smugglers Lane; or to moorings from Deep End to Birdham: 1000–1800 on every even hour. Details from the Harbour Office at which other ferry trips can sometimes be arranged.

14.13.    Bosham Quay.


14.12.    (Left) Verner beacon half way up the Emsworth Channel, and (right) Marker beacon just off
Marker Point in the Emsworth Channel.

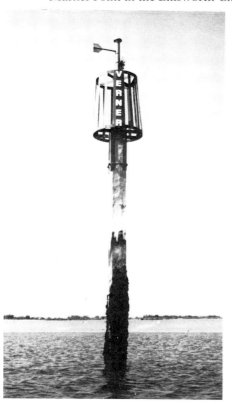

**Facilities.** At Itchenor there are excellent facilities as it is the home port of cruising yachts of all kinds and it is a notable dinghy and small class racing centre, based on the very active Itchenor SC. There are several yacht yards and fuel is available. Launching site at hard. Water at the jetty.

At the picturesque Dell Quay there is the sailing club, J K Marine (Dell Quay) Ltd, Wyche Marine Ltd, an inn with restaurant, and 20 minutes' walk to shops and garage. It is possible to dry out alongside the end of the quay on hard bottom, but mud on N and S of quay. Public hard north of quay. Moorings for shoal draught craft may be available on application at yacht yards but they all dry out. It may be of interest to add that in the late Roman era the Fishbourne Channel was much deeper and big ships came right up to Fishbourne, a mile west of Chichester. The excavations of the palace of the British vassal king, consisting of a rectangle round a courtyard, reconstructed gardens and quays where the ships tied up, are open to the public.

Bosham also caters well for yachtsmen. It is possible for a yacht to dry out alongside the quay (by permission of the Quay Master) where there is the Bosham SC. Launching site at quay or street end. Several yacht and boatyards supply water, fuel and chandlery. Water at

14.14.   Emsworth Beacon is a south Cardinal mark $(Q\,(6)+LFl\;15s)$. The channel is between the lines of yachts.

14.15.    Fisherman's Beacon on the middle ground where the Emsworth Channel divides near
            Fowley Island.

Bosham quay. In the village there are shops and a PO. EC Thursday. Buses to Chichester
and Portsmouth.

### The Emsworth Channel

The Emsworth Channel is a straight, broad, deep, well marked fairway as far as its
junction with Sweare Deep and, with sufficient rise of tide, it continues navigable up to
Emsworth, where there is a yacht harbour and excellent facilities. With the aid of the lights
referred to below, navigation is now possible at night under suitable conditions.

The channel is entered between Sandy Point and the Fishery buoy (*Q (6) + LFl 15s*). A
line of yachts on moorings will lie on the port hand and to starboard the green NW Pilsey
buoy (*Fl G 5s*). The next mark is the green N Pilsey buoy, followed on the port hand by the
red can buoy marking the entrance to Mill Rythe. About a quarter of a mile north of this
and also on the port hand is Verner beacon (*Fl R 10s*). Just over half a mile further are
Marker Point and the Marker beacon (*Fl (2) G 10s*).

About three quarters of a mile beyond Marker Point is the junction where Sweare Deep
joins the main channel to Emsworth. Between the two channels lies a large expanse of mud
flats intersected by creeks and covered at HW except for the small Fowley Island, which is
little more than two disused salterns surmounted by a sea wall.

On the port hand the NE Hayling beacon (*Fl (2) R 10s*) marks the bend to the north-west
into Sweare Deep. A little further north and marking the middle ground of the junction of

the two channels is the South Cardinal Emsworth Beacon (*Q (6) + L Fl 15s*). This prominent beacon is at the end of a line of pile moorings or trots along the west side of the Emsworth channel (see photograph on page 131). The Emsworth Beacon also carries a tide gauge indicating the depth of water over the sill at the Yacht Harbour. The fairway is clearly indicated by the moorings. About half a mile further up from the Emsworth Beacon is Fisherman's Beacon (*Fl (3) R 10s*). This is almost abreast of Fowley Island and marks the junction of three narrow creeks. The one on the port hand is Fowley Rythe and has 1.2 to 0.6 m at CD for a short distance, in which there are yachts on moorings. The starboard hand creek is Little Deep, and has at least 1 m for nearly a quarter of a mile on ordinary tides at LW, with moorings for local yachts of shallow draught.

The principal creek between the two continues up to Emsworth. It becomes narrow and shallow and runs almost parallel to Fisherman's Walk, a long hard over the mud from Emsworth almost to Fowley Rythe which dries about 2 hours either side of LW, and has a notice board at its end. The channel is marked a further half a mile on by Echo Beacon (*Fl (3) G 10s*). The wrecks that used to be a feature here have been removed. The creek divides again at Echo Beacon, the port hand creek leading to Emsworth quay and the other to Tarquin Yacht Harbour. The channel is very narrow but marked by perches. The sill at the entrance is 2.1 m so the depth above it at HW is approximately the Portsmouth height less 2 m. For example, if the Portsmouth tide table shows a tide of 4.3 m there will be about 2.2 m on the sill.

The following are creeks on the west side of the Emsworth Channel in order from the entrance:

**Mengham Rythe:** The entrance to this creek is north of Sandy Point and has an east Cardinal perch with tide gauge placed high on the mud flats on the starboard side. The channel is marked by perches but the yachts on moorings in the centre are the best guide to its direction. Less than half a mile from the entrance there is a junction. The port hand creek leads to Eastoke and Sparkes Yacht Harbour (just west of Sandy Point). It is marked by port and starboard hand beacons and carries 2 m at MLWS as far as the Yacht Harbour. The main channel bears NW and continues to be 1.8 to 2.4 m deep until it bends to the SW after which it becomes very narrow and soon dries out. The upper reach is navigable by dinghies and craft of shoal draught and leads to Salterns Quay and Mengham Rythe Sailing Club, which has a week-end bar. There is a hard and boatyard and ½ mile distant is Mengham village, with PO, garage and shops.

**Mill Rythe:** The entrance to this creek lies about three quarters of a mile north of Mengham Rythe. It is marked on the south side by the red can Mill Rythe buoy which, as mentioned, is a port hand buoy for the main Emsworth Channel, and on the mud on the north side by an east Cardinal perch. The creek is marked by perches, red can tops port, green triangles starboard.

14.16.   The channel to Langstone Bridge, showing two east Cardinal perches (one has had a knock!) that are left to starboard.

For the first quarter of a mile the bottom is uneven, and briefly dries out 0.3 m at CD before deepening and widening with from 0.3 to 1.5 m as far as the remains of the pier at Wall Corner. It then dries out again and divides into two winding creeks, the northern one leading to Yachthaven and the southern to Hayling Yacht Co Ltd, which can be reached with sufficient rise of tide. Facilities at yacht yards. PO, shop and bus stop half a mile inland.

**Sweare Deep:** This wide channel runs from its junction with the Emsworth Channel in a NW direction between extensive mud banks. It is entered by leaving to port the NE Hayling beacon (*Fl (2) R 10s*). There is often a round orange racing buoy moored near the entrance. Sweare Deep has increased in significance since the opening of the Northney Marina and is clearly marked by the Sweare Deep Beacon (*Fl (3) R 10s*) half a mile up on the port hand, and by the Northney beacon (*Fl (4) R 10s*) about a quarter of a mile on at the entrance to the short dredged channel to the marina. The channel is also marked by perches (red can to port; green triangle to starboard). There is a least depth of 1.2 m as far as the Sweare Deep Beacon and much of it is 1.8 to 2.4 m. There are oyster beds on the starboard side of the channel with 'Keep Off' notices. Sweare Deep is well sheltered from SW winds and, although there are many moorings, it provides a good anchorage but rather remote from facilities.

**Northney Marina.** There is a dredged channel with a least depth of 1 m from Northney Beacon (*Fl (4) R 10s*) into the marina basin. Details of the facilities available at all the marinas in Chichester Harbour will be found in Appendix 2.

Beyond this the channel divides into three, all of which dry out at CD. There are two East Cardinal perches on the middle grounds between the branches of the channel, two

14.17. Northney Beacon (*Fl (4) R (102)*), and the entrance to Northney Marina.

going north west, the main one west, and there is also often a round orange racing buoy in the channel between the perches.

The westerly arm leads to Langstone Bridge and thence to Langstone Harbour. When entering this channel leave the East Cardinal perch to starboard and the line of small yachts on moorings to port. Once past the entrance to the channel the rest is easy, as although narrow and shallow it is well marked by perches. Near the bridge is the West Cuts West Cardinal beacon to be left to port when proceeding west.

The entrances to the two NW arms are separated by the more easterly of the two East Cardinal perches already mentioned. These arms join again about a quarter of a mile on where the middle ground is further marked by a west Cardinal perch. The channel then continues in a semi-circular bend to Langstone village and sailing club, and finally south to join the other arm near Langstone Bridge.

At Langstone village there is Langstone Sailing Club and The Ship Inn, with car park and public hard (launching site when room) adjacent at the NE end of bridge. The hard on the NW is leased to the sailing club. Buses to Havant and Hayling. There is a dinghy hard and park at Duckard Point on the south side of the channel a quarter of a mile east of the bridge, where land reclamation is in progress.

### Moorings, Anchorage and Facilities

Emsworth is an important yachting centre and there is anchorage in the Emsworth Channel and associated creeks anywhere clear of moorings, cables and the fishery areas (marked by notice boards on perches) mostly on the east bank of the channel. The Harbour Master's office is at Itchenor, and the whole of Chichester Harbour, including Emsworth, is centred under his authority. There are innumerable moorings within the area which are privately rented and application should be made to the Harbour Master or at the Yacht Harbour to ascertain whether any are temporarily vacant.

There are scrubbing piles at Emsworth, just off the sea wall, and at Itchenor beside the hard. Apply to the Harbour Master.

The principal base in the Emsworth Channel is the Tarquin Yacht Harbour. The surroundings are not picturesque, but the facilities are good. Associated with the yacht harbour is a yacht yard, marine engineers, shop with chandlery, brokerage, car park, slipways, fuelling jetty and water. Emsworth has all the usual facilities of a small town. EC Wednesday. Station and good bus service.

# Appendices

## 1    Marinas in the Solent Area – Facilities

| MARINAS | Permanent berths | Visitors' berths | VHF Watch/Channel | Access at all states of the tide | Diesel | Petrol | Water (to berths) | Electricity (to berths) | Toilets/showers | Laundrette | Bar/restaurant | Chandlery | Haulage/Cranage | Yard repairs | Ice | Provisions |
|---|---|---|---|---|---|---|---|---|---|---|---|---|---|---|---|---|
| **Lymington** | | | | | | | | | | | | | | | | |
| Lymington Yacht Haven    (0509) 677071 | 575 | 100 | 37/80 | Yes | • | • | • | • | • | • | = | • | • | • | • | = |
| Berthon Lymington Marina    (0590) 673312 | 300 | 100 | 37 | Yes | • | • | • | • | = | = | = | = | • | • | • | = |
| **Beaulieu River** | | | | | | | | | | | | | | | | |
| Buckler's Hard Yacht Harbour    (0590) 616200 | 110 | 20+ | No | Yes | • | • | • | • | • | • | • | • | • | • | • | • |
| **Cowes and Medina River** | | | | | | | | | | | | | | | | |
| West Cowes Marina    (0983) 295724 | 50 | 200 | 37/80 | Yes | • | = | • | • | • | = | = | • | = | = | • | = |
| Cowes Marina (0983)    293983 | 120 | 150 | 80 | Yes | = | = | • | = | • | = | • | • | • | • | • | • |
| Island Harbour Marina    (0983) 822999 | 240 | % | 37 | No | • | • | • | = | • | • | @ | • | @ | • | • | @ |
| **Southampton Water** | | | | | | | | | | | | | | | | |
| Hythe Marina Village    (0703) 207073 | 210 | .% | 80 | No | • | • | • | • | • | • | • | • | • | • | • | • |
| Town Quay Marina    (0703) 234397 – Due for completion 1992/3 | | | | | | | | | | | | | | | | |
| Ocean Village Marina    (0703) 229385 | 400 | % | 80 | Yes | = | = | • | • | • | • | = | • | × | × | • | • |
| Shamrock Quay Marina    (0703) 229461 | 250 | % | 80 | Yes | = | × | • | • | • | • | • | • | • | • | = | • |
| Kemps Quay Marina    (0703) 632323 | 220 | % | No | No | = | = | = | = | • | = | • | = | • | = | = | = |
| **Hamble River** | | | | | | | | | | | | | | | | |
| Hamble Point Marina    (0703) 452464 | 190 | % | 80 | Yes | • | = | • | • | • | • | • | • | • | • | • | • |
| Port Hamble Marina    (0703) 452741 | 300 | 60 | 80 | Yes | • | • | • | • | • | • | • | • | • | • | • | • |
| Mercury Yacht Harbour    (0703) 455994 | 346 | % | 80 | Yes | = | = | • | • | • | • | • | • | • | • | = | • |
| Universal Shipyards (Solent) Ltd    (0489) 574272 | 91 | % | 37 | Yes | = | = | • | = | • | = | • | • | • | • | • | = |
| Swanwick Marina (A H Moody & Son)    (0489) 885000 | 375 | % | 80 | Yes | • | • | • | • | • | = | • | • | • | • | • | • |
| **Portsmouth Harbour** | | | | | | | | | | | | | | | | |
| Camper & Nicholsons Marina    (0705) 524811 | 380 | 40 | 37/80 | Yes | • | • | • | • | • | • | • | • | • | • | • | • |
| **Fareham and Portchester Lakes** | | | | | | | | | | | | | | | | |
| Fareham Marine    (0329) 822445 | 55 | % | 37 | No | • | • | • | • | = | = | = | • | = | = | × | = |
| Port Solent Marina    (0705) 210765 | 850 | 50+ | 80 | Yes | • | • | • | • | • | • | • | • | • | • | • | • |
| **Bembridge Harbour** | | | | | | | | | | | | | | | | |
| Bembridge Marina    (0983) 872828 | 50 | 100 | 37–80 | No | = | = | • | = | • | × | = | = | = | = | = | = |
| **Langstone Harbour** | | | | | | | | | | | | | | | | |
| Langstone Marina    (0705) 822719 | 320 | 30 | 37–80 | No | • | = | • | • | @ | @ | • | • | • | • | • | • |
| **Chichester Harbour** | | | | | | | | | | | | | | | | |
| Sparkes Yacht Harbour    (0705) 463572 | 150 | 35 | 37 | Yes | • | • | • | • | • | • | • | • | • | • | • | • |
| Northney Marina    (0705) 466321 | 228 | 10 | 80 | Yes | • | = | • | • | • | × | • | × | • | • | × | = |
| Tarquin Yacht Harbour    (0243) 375211 | 200 | 60+ | 37/80 | No | • | • | • | • | • | = | = | • | • | • | = | = |
| Birdham Shipyard Ltd    (0243) 512310 | 230 | % | No | No | • | • | • | • | = | × | = | • | • | • | = | = |
| Chichester Yacht Basin    (0243) 512731 | 1071 | 40 | 37 | No | • | • | • | = | • | • | • | • | • | • | • | • |

% According to availability

• On site/all berths

= Within half a mile/some berths

× Not available

@ Available soon

137

## 2   DECCA Systems

| PRESENTATION OF LONGITUDE AND LATITUDE | | |
|---|---|---|
| | *Latitude* | *Longitude* |
| RACAL DECCA III | N 49:48.72 | W 4:00.70 |
| RACAL DECCA IV | 49:48.18 N | 4:00.89 W |
| Navstar 2000D | N 52:57.6 | W 1:10.97 |
| Vigil RX | 51 26.97 N | 0 56.08 W |
| Shipmate 4001 | 56°52.15 N | 0°46.35 E |
| Shipmate 4100 | 54°56.12 N | 10°32.19 E |

## 3   Waypoints: Approaches to the Solent

| Western Approaches | Lat N ° ′ | | Long W ° ′ | |
|---|---|---|---|---|
| *Fairway* buoy RW | | | | |
| L Fl 10s – Horn(1)10s | 50 | 38.20 | 01 | 38.90 |
| *Christchurch Ledge* (S car) buoy YB | 50 | 40.97 | 01 | 41.69 |
| *Bridge* (W car) buoy YBY VQ(9)10s | 50 | 39.59 | 01 | 36.80 |
| *Wave Research Structure* | 50 | 42.87 | 01 | 38.25 |
| Mo(U)Wr 15s 10m 5M | | | | |
| *NE Shingles* (E car) buoy BYB VQ(3)5s | 50 | 41.93 | 01 | 33.32 |
| *North Head* buoy G Fl(3)G 10s | 50 | 42.65 | 01 | 35.42 |

| Eastern Approaches | | | | |
|---|---|---|---|---|
| *Nab Tower* | 50 | 40.10 | 01 | 57.05 |
| Fl 10s 20M & Fl R 10s 14M | | | | |
| *Warner* buoy R QR | 50 | 43.83 | 01 | 03.91 |
| *Bembridge Ledge* (E Car) buoy BYB Q3 | 50 | 41.15 | 01 | 02.70 |
| *No Man's Land Fort* Fl 5s | 50 | 44.40 | 01 | 05.60 |
| *Horse Sand Fort* Fl G 2 5s | 50 | 45.00 | 01 | 04.25 |

| | Lat N | | Long W | |
|---|---|---|---|---|
| **Keyhaven** | ° | ′ | ° | ′ |
| *Hurst* anchorage | 50 | 42.55 | 01 | 32.80 |
| *North Point* | 50 | 42.80 | 01 | 33.13 |
| | | | | |
| **Yarmouth** | | | | |
| *Sconce* (N Car) buoy BY Q | 50 | 42.50 | 01 | 31.35 |
| *Yarmouth Pier* 2FR (vert) | 50 | 42.50 | 01 | 29.9 |
| | | | | |
| **Lymington River** | | | | |
| *Jack-in-the-Basket* beacon Fl R 2s | 50 | 44.25 | 01 | 30.50 |
| | | | | |
| **Newtown River** | | | | |
| *Hamstead Ledge* buoy G F(2)G 5s | 50 | 43.80 | 01 | 26.00 |
| *Bar* buoy R | 50 | 43.75 | 01 | 24.82 |
| *Salt Mead* buoy G Fl(3) G 10s | 50 | 44.49 | 01 | 22.94 |
| | | | | |
| **Beaulieu River** | | | | |
| *East Lepe* buoy R Fl(2)R 5s | 50 | 46.08 | 01 | 20.81 |
| *Stone point* (western) beacon QR | 50 | 46.73 | 01 | 20.73 |
| *Dolphin* marking entrance QR | 50 | 46.84 | 01 | 21.68 |
| | | | | |
| **Medina River** | | | | |
| *Gurnard* (N Car) buoy BY Q | 50 | 46.18 | 01 | 18.76 |
| *Prince Consort* (N Car) buoy BY VQ | 50 | 46.40 | 01 | 17.50 |
| *No 4 buoy* R R Fl R | 50 | 46.04 | 01 | 17.80 |

## Southampton Water – Western Approach

| | Lat | N | Long | W |
|---|---|---|---|---|
| | ° | ′ | ° | ′ |
| *Stone Point* (western beacon) | 50 | 46.73 | 01 | 20.73 |
| *East Lepe* buoy R Fl(2)R 5s | 50 | 46.08 | 01 | 20.72 |
| *NE Gurnard* buoy R Fl(3)R 10s | 50 | 47.50 | 01 | 19.34 |
| *Bourne Gap* buoy R Fl R 3s | 50 | 47.80 | 01 | 18.25 |
| *Calshot Spit* light float Fl 5s | 50 | 48.32 | 01 | 17.56 |
| *Castle Point* buoy R IQ R 10s | 50 | 48.73 | 01 | 17.57 |
| *Black Jack* buoy R Fl(2)R 4s | 50 | 49.10 | 01 | 18.00 |

## Southampton Water – Eastern Approach

| | Lat | N | Long | W |
|---|---|---|---|---|
| *Hillhead* buoy R Fl R 2 5s | 50 | 48 04 | 01 | 15.91 |
| *Calshot* (N Car) buoy By VQ | 50 | 48.40 | 01 | 16.98 |
| *Coronation* buoy Y Fl Y 5s | 50 | 49.50 | 01 | 17.54 |
| *Hamble Point* (S Car) buoy YB Q(6) + LF 15s | 50 | 50.10 | 01 | 18.56 |

## Southampton Water – West side of big ship channel

| | Lat | N | Long | W |
|---|---|---|---|---|
| *Fawley Jetty* (S end) 2FR (vert) | 50 | 50.05 | 01 | 19.35 |
| *Cadland* buoy R Fl R 3s | 50 | 50.99 | 01 | 20.45 |
| *Lains Lake* buoy R Fl(2) R 4s | 50 | 51.54 | 01 | 21.57 |
| *Deans Elbow* buoy R Occ R 4s | 50 | 52.13 | 01 | 22.69 |
| *Hythe Pier* 2FR (vert) | 50 | 52.46 | 01 | 23.51 |
| *Hythe Knock* buoy R Fl R 3s | 50 | 52.78 | 01 | 27.72 |

## Hythe Marina entrance channel

| | Lat | N | Long | W |
|---|---|---|---|---|
| *Gymp* buoy R QR | 50 | 53.14 | 01 | 24.22 |
| *Gymp Elbow* buoy R Occ R 4s | 50 | 53.48 | 01 | 24.54 |
| *Swinging Ground* No 2 buoy R Fl(2) R 10s | 50 | 53.78 | 01 | 25.03 |
| *Swinging Ground* No 4 buoy R Occ R 4s | 50 | 54.16 | 01 | 25.80 |
| *Bury* buoy R Fl R 5s | 50 | 54.10 | 01 | 27.20 |
| *Swinging Ground* No 10 buoy R QR | 50 | 54.26 | 01 | 27.41 |
| *Eling* buoy R Fl R 5s | 50 | 54.45 | 01 | 27.75 |

## Southampton Water – East side of big ship channel

| | Lat N | | Long W | |
|---|---|---|---|---|
| | ° | ′ | ° | ′ |
| *Hamble Point* (S Car) buoy YB Q(6) + LF 15s | 50 | 50.12 | 01 | 18.56 |
| *Shell Jetty* 2FR (vert) | 50 | 50.80 | 01 | 19.46 |
| *Greenland* buoy G IQ G 10s | 50 | 51.10 | 01 | 20.29 |
| *Hound* buoy G Fl(3) G 10s | 50 | 51.67 | 01 | 21.46 |
| *NW Netley* buoy G Fl G 7s | 50 | 50.27 | 01 | 22.62 |
| *Weston Shelf* buoy G Fl (3) G 15s | 50 | 52.67 | 01 | 23.15 |
| *Swinging Ground* No 1 buoy G Occ G 4s | 50 | 52.97 | 01 | 23.35 |

## Hamble River

| | Lat N | | Long W | |
|---|---|---|---|---|
| *Hamble Point* (S Car) buoy YB Q(6) + LF 15s | 50 | 50.10 | 01 | 18.56 |
| *Pile No 1* G Fl G 2s | 50 | 50.31 | 01 | 18.57 |

## Titchfield Haven (Hill Head)

| | Lat N | | Long W | |
|---|---|---|---|---|
| *Hillhead* buoy R Fl R 2 5s | 50 | 48.04 | 01 | 15.93 |
| *Haven entrance* | 50 | 49.03 | 01 | 14.42 |

## Wootton Creek

| | Lat N | | Long W | |
|---|---|---|---|---|
| *Peel Bank* buoy R Fl(2) R 5s | 50 | 45.58 | 01 | 13.30 |
| *Mother Bank* buoy R Fl R 3s | 50 | 45.44 | 01 | 11.12 |
| *Ryde Pier* 2FR (vert) | 50 | 44.35 | 01 | 9.48 |
| *Wootton Beacon* (N Car) BY Q | 50 | 44.45 | 01 | 12.09 |
| *No 1 beacon* G Fl G 3s | 50 | 44.30 | 01 | 12.30 |

## Portsmouth Harbour entrance – from the East

| | Lat N | | Long W | |
|---|---|---|---|---|
| *Horse Sand Fort* Fl G 2 5s | 50 | 45.00 | 01 | 04.25 |
| *Main Passage* (through barrier) QR | 50 | 45.97 | 01 | 04.01 |
| *Boat Passage* (through barrier) | 50 | 46.65 | 01 | 04.05 |
| *Spit Refuge* buoy R Fl R 5s | 50 | 46.12 | 01 | 05.38 |
| *Spit Sand Fort* Fl R 5s | 50 | 46.20 | 01 | 05.85 |

|  | Lat N | | Long W | |
|---|---|---|---|---|
|  | ° | ′ | ° | ′ |
| *No 2 buoy* R Fl(3) R 10s | 50 | 46.66 | 01 | 05.85 |
| *No 4 buoy* R QR | 50 | 46.97 | 01 | 06.27 |
| *Fort Blockhouse* NB 2FR (vert) | 50 | 47.35 | 01 | 06.62 |

### Portsmouth Harbour – from the West

| *Gilkicker Point* (2 cables S) Occ G 10s | 50 | 46.20 | 01 | 08.18 |
|---|---|---|---|---|

### Portsmouth Harbour – from the South

| *N Sturbridge* (N Car) buoy BY VQ | 50 | 45.30 | 01 | 08.15 |
|---|---|---|---|---|

### Bembridge Harbour

| *St Helens Fort* Fl(3) 10s 16m 8M | 50 | 42.27 | 01 | 4.95 |
|---|---|---|---|---|
| *Tide Gauge* beacon Fl Y 2s | 50 | 42.55 | 01 | 5.23 |

### Langstone Harbour

| *Roway Wreck* beacon BRB Fl(2) 5s | 50 | 46.07 | 01 | 2.20 |
|---|---|---|---|---|
| *Langstone Fairway* buoy RW L Fl 10s | 50 | 46.28 | 01 | 01.25 |
| Beacon at west side of entrance QR | 50 | 47.2 | 01 | 01.06 |

### Chichester Harbour

| *Chi Spit* buoy R | 50 | 45.68 | 01 | 56.47 |
|---|---|---|---|---|
| *Chichester Bar* beacon RW Fl WR 5s | 50 | 45.88 | 01 | 56.36 |
| *W Winner* tide gauge and beacon G QG | 50 | 46.84 | 01 | 55.89 |